# How to
# think about
# the Earth

# How to think about the Earth

## Philosophical and theological models for ecology

..................................................

## Stephen R. L. Clark

MOWBRAY

Mowbray
A Cassell imprint
Villiers House, 41/47 Strand, London WC2N 5JE
387 Park Avenue South, New York, NY 10016–8810

First published 1993

British Library Cataloguing-in-Publication Data
A catalogue record for this book is available from the British
Library.

Library of Congress Cataloging-in-Publication Data
Clark, Stephen R. L.
    How to think about the earth / Stephen R. L. Clark.
        p.      cm.
    ISBN 0–264–67304–2
        1. Earth—Religious aspects.      2. Human ecology—
Religious aspects.      3. Goddess religion.      4. National
socialism—Religious aspects.      5. Process philosophy.      I.
Title.
BL226.C57   1994
291.1'78362—dc20                                               93–7921
                                                                CIP

ISBN 0–264–67304–2

Phototypeset by Intype, London
Printed and bound in Great Britain by
Mackays of Chatham plc

# Contents

# Acknowledgements

The author gratefully acknowledges the permission of the following to include copyright material in this book: Faber and Faber Ltd and Random House, Inc., for two lines from W. H. Auden, 'Words', © 1960, and two lines from his 'Memorial for the City', in *Collected Shorter Poems 1926–56*, ed. E. Mendelson, © 1976 executors of the Estate of W. H. Auden; Faber and Faber Ltd and Oxford University Press, New York, for twenty lines from E. Muir's 'The Transfiguration'; Random House, Inc., for fourteen lines from R. Jeffers' 'The Double Axe', two from his 'Extinct Vertebrate', nine from 'The Answer' and three from 'The Redeemer'.

# Preface

When I was asked to deliver the Scott Holland lectures for 1992, I seized the occasion to express my worries about a good deal of modern environmentalist rhetoric. This does not mean either that I doubt the severity of our crisis, or that I reject modern environmentalism as worthless. On the contrary, it is because I do think there is a crisis, and that the preachers whose words I attempt to dissect are groping after important truths that I think it is vital to exercise a discriminating judgement in these matters. In preparing my lectures, of course, I grew ever more conscious of how much there was to read on the subject, and how much specialist knowledge, in a variety of different disciplines, was needed. I have taken a narrow view of the problem for this very reason. There are people whose work I have not discussed, and issues in economics, bacteriology and history that I cannot sensibly discuss. The answers to our problems may well lie in details, in 'minute particulars'. There is still some room for sympathetic, but critical, analysis of the larger claims made by preachers, lobbyists and politicians.

Some parts of these lectures have been tried out elsewhere, within my department, at Lancaster University and Bowling Green State University. I am grateful to my auditors and critics there, to the Scott Holland Trustees (especially Professor Ronald Preston), and to the staff of St Katherine's College, Liverpool, where the lectures were delivered. I must also thank Gillian Clark, Paul Helm, Michael McGhee, Lourdes McGunigle, Howard Robinson and Mark Sacks for their advice and assistance over the last several, trying, years. Much of the reading for the lectures was completed during a brief stay at All Souls College, during the summer of 1991. I am grateful to the Warden and Fellows for allowing me the time, and to my family for putting up with my physical absence then, and my absence-of-mind thereafter.

No one should expect that what follows is disengaged analysis. Philosophers as much as poets wish to open their (our) eyes and ears to what is done and undone. We wish to see things clearly and to see them whole, partly because there is so much to see of beauty, and partly because we see no other hope of finding our way through the tangles of our life on earth. What follows is in the ancient tradition of philosophical diatribe, but I hope I have avoided any hectoring or abusive manner (except, of course, when voicing the opinions of hectoring or abusive angels). Addicts are rarely altered by abuse: since all of us are addicts, what we need is a new vision of real beauty, and the opportunity to live 'in beauty'. I hope they come in time.

4 March 1993

# The roots of our environmental crisis

## A A religion for the times?

The social and environmental problems that we face at this tail end of twentieth-century progress require us to identify some cause, some spirit that transcends the petty limits of our time and place, that gives us something to work for that is not just 'our own profit'. Any one of us can all too easily be convinced that things will last our time, and dedicate ourselves to enjoying things while we can. Fortunately for the future, and our children's fortunes, most of us do identify with our posterity, plant woodlands that we shall not see, and seek to save our children's children from disaster. Once people are convinced that the natural world can no longer be taken for granted as the unchanging context for our ups and downs, some action follows. But our willingness to sacrifice our own present interests for the general good of humankind or of the world is feeble: advising others not to cut down rain forests or pollute the seas is easy enough; preserving our own wetlands or cutting back on burgers is another matter. Only a 'religious spirit', a willed and eager commitment to a larger whole, can easily sustain us through adversity, let alone through prosperity. The question is: what spirit shall that be?

Arnold Toynbee, conversing with Daisatsu Ikeda in the early seventies, declared a right religion is one that teaches respect for the dignity and sanctity of all nature. The wrong religion is one that licenses the indulgence of human greed at the expense of non-human nature. I conclude that the religion we need to embrace now is pantheism, as exemplified in Shinto, and that the religion we now need to discard is Judaic monotheism and the post-Christian non-theistic faith in scientific progress, which has inherited from Christianity the belief that mankind is morally entitled to exploit the rest of the universe for the indulgence of human greed.[1]

I share Toynbee's belief that a crisis is upon us, but wish to argue that pantheism in all its forms is exactly what we do not need, and that Christian faith, along with the other great religions of the Book, does already teach respect for the dignity and sanctity of God's creation. The attitudes he criticizes are actually unChristian, and unJewish.

I shall explore and criticize such contemporary models for an environmentally-conscious theology as Goddess-worship, polytheism, National Socialism, and process philosophy, and argue that a more resolutely orthodox approach has greater strength and subtlety than is usually acknowledged. My aim throughout has been to understand, and make good cases for, the models that have been offered. The words that follow, therefore, are not always to be heard as mine. I doubt if I can really conceal my prejudices or my final judgements from attentive readers, but experience tells me that there will always be a few who mistake my opponent's creed for mine. One further difficulty for readers must be that I cannot always distinguish doctrines that are intended as straightforward descriptions of a metaphysical reality from ones that are intended rather as poetic advice to feel and act in one way or another. I cannot do so, because many of those whose words and arguments I am relaying don't do so. A religious utterance, in one mouth, may be an attempt at Truth; in another, it may be only 'let's pretend'; in a third, it may be serious, encoded policy. Some take the Goddess seriously as what there really is; some speak of Her so as to suggest new ways of humane living. Some think that we can find out truths about God; others (even the same thinkers in another mood) that we can only learn to obey what we can't understand; others (or the same) that 'God' stands only for our highest dreams. Exploration in this area is always difficult. I think, nonetheless, that there are some landmarks mapped, and that some pathways lead to cliffs or bogs. Explorers can expect to find things that surprise them, but they should not therefore throw away such maps or compasses as they have found before. In brief, as I remark upon a later page, we may need a new religion, but we certainly need to keep our wits about us when we are offered one.

Arguments about the moral or political programmes encapsulated in this religious dream or that will always be difficult especially because they almost always beg the question. It is no answer to some novel proposal that it conflicts with older nostrums: obviously it does. But there are older principles that we would be ill-advised to abandon, whatever the attraction of the new. It is a pious hope that really wicked policies will quickly reveal their inner contradictions: I doubt if we can be sure that there is really only one coherent moral system (fortunately identical with fashionably liberal prejudice). We may sometimes have to admit that 'here we stand: we can do no other', that *this* is the voice of God, in effect, to us. My own suspicion is that this stance is not rationally possible for fashionably materialist thinkers (though any may be better than their principles require).

Arguments about metaphysical truth (or even, sometimes, readily experienced truth) are also difficult, not least because it is easy to think that *we* are only reporting *facts*, and *they* report mere fictions. Merely to state the Truth, we think, will instantly persuade all but mere fools or knaves. I have encountered this assumption amongst Muslims, Christians, born-again atheists and, of course, myself. It is not true, even though we have Blake's word for it that 'truth can never be told *so as to be understood*, and not be believ'd'.[2] Even when we begin to argue, it is all too easy, as before, to beg the question. Any argument that leads to an unwelcome end is reckoned invalid – even if we have to identify a hitherto unknown fallacy to avoid defeat. Our opponents' theses are judged on the 'highest standard', while we cheerfully concede – in private – that there are often occasions when we cannot see how our own theses can be true together (as we think they are). Until we are all omniscient, errors will accumulate. Sometimes we must simply trust our mortal judgement in advance of any final proof (on which more below).

In matters metaphysical, and especially religious, the problem gets still worse. Merely to say 'religious' annoys some people beyond bearing; merely to say it misleads others into thinking one is talking about 'religions' as they understand their own. Not all religious utterance is metaphysical; not all is theological; not all is monotheistic; rather little of it is – so to call it – Abrahamic.[3] When I speak of 'God' in the pages following the context will provide most clues to exactly what I am speaking of. But as a general rule, and almost till the end, nothing I say is peculiar to the forms of theism identifiable as

Abrahamic. More often than not (as often in my books before) I am speaking of 'God' as pagan Platonists did, and often in ways that I could fairly easily translate into less theological modes.

## B Making believe

It is easy to believe that there is no crisis. We have been told too often that the oceans will soon die, the air be poisonous, our energy reserves run dry; that the world will grow warmer, coastlands be flooded and the climate change; that plague, famine and war will be the necessary checks on population growth. But here we are: sufficiently healthy and well-fed, connoisseurs of far-off catastrophe and horror movies, sublimely confident that something will turn up or that the prophecies of doom were only dreams. We are the descendants, after all, of creatures who did not despair, who hoped against hope that there would still be life tomorrow. We cannot believe in absolute disaster, especially if we can think it's been postponed. We no more believe in world's end than we believe that soldiers could break down the door and drag us off to torture and to death; we don't *believe* that they could even when we know that, somewhere altogether elsewhere, they did that. Even if we can force ourselves to remember other ages, other lands or other classes, we are content enough.

> There is one creed: 'neath no world-terror's wing
> Apples forget to grow on apple-trees.[4]

The resilience of those who cannot believe in cataclysmic change is reinforced by images of seasonal adjustment and return. Such changes as we can make ourselves admit are bound to be temporary: only oscillations within a larger quiet. We come to expect heart-warming panics: every few years we are reminded of the abstract possibility of nuclear spasm, poisoned water, global warming, meteor strikes, solar flares and rabid foxes. We shiver delightfully, glad to be distracted from our real concerns: mortgages and family relationships and the little lump we just discovered and who left the fridge door open. We shiver, but we know, or firmly believe, that the panic will subside, the threat seem far away, and even if it were to happen, still things would go on. Nature at least is immortal, and our civilization, even though we can give no reason for our confidence, seems to us to be entirely natural. Even to suggest otherwise is at once absurd and impolite: it almost seems that we suspect that speaking makes things so. Of course, we think, such changes are impossible, but talking about them might encourage them to happen. I shall have more to say about this residual belief in magic.

So none of us can quite believe there is a crisis, or cannot believe it long. Nonetheless, I am, in the abstract, fairly sure there is, and that the crisis cannot be resolved without a change more radical than I can quite imagine. My effort in this book will not be to make your flesh creep, or mine. The literature on the dangers facing us, that we can't face, must already have cut down several forests. It has had some effect, at an immediately practical level and in altering deep-seated attitudes, at least among those with time and cash to spare.

> For generations, we have assumed that the efforts of mankind would leave the fundamental equilibrium of the world's systems and atmosphere stable. But it is possible that with all these enormous changes (population, agricultural, use of fossil fuels) concentrated into such a short period of time, we have unwittingly begun a massive experiment with the system of this planet itself.[5]

Maybe the prophets of doom will soon be reduced to Jonah's state, grumpily conscious that the worst will not occur, because enough of us did, after all, 'turn from our wickedness and live'. Or maybe they won't. The details of the dangers, real or fantasized, I shall not rehearse. Nor shall I do more than hint at some of the political consequences of the changes I endorse: I have in the past described myself as an 'anarcho-conservative', but 'agrarian populist' or 'distributist' might serve as well.[6] I wish instead to talk about those alterations in religious consciousness that the prophets urge on us.

The question must at once be raised: why should we need any? If it is true that we are using up irreplaceable resources, dumping waste into our land, air and water faster than any natural processes can cope with them, and seeking to spread an American bourgeois life-style through an expanding population, then it seems to require little prophetic insight or religious experience to suspect the worst. Once we realize what we are doing we will take appropriate steps. Or else perhaps we won't, especially since it is difficult to specify those steps in a way that is both hopeful and conservative: technological fixes, there is some reason to suspect, only delay things. We are, as I declared before, creatures bred to ignore uncomfortable truths, or to make them harmless by deploring them. Even if we can be brought to believe the rumours, we shall not really assent to them, any more than other addicts make their fears real to themselves.[7] No one supposes that an alcoholic will be cured by mouthing slogans against alcohol. Something like a religious experience may be necessary: by which I only mean that some episode – as it might be, a child killed by a drunken driver – may suddenly ignite us to a real assent, not just a notional. Such an experience, a waking-up to what we knew, or believed, already is recognizably 'religious' when the beliefs are such, and maybe more beliefs are really religious than we suppose. Why should a *child*'s death strike us so acutely?

It is perhaps necessary to pause for a moment on that word 'religious'. Some of us are so acutely conscious of the evils performed in the name of 'religion' and so suspicious of 'religious' theories, as to find it unthinkable that anyone could really wish for a 'religious awakening'. It is an axiom, for them, that 'religion' equals ignorance and superstition. We should be glad to be rid of priestcraft, and speak out against any and all attempts to popularize the thing. What we need instead is knowledge (of the global setting) and determination (to achieve such obvious goals as security against disease, invasion and starvation). But those who say this sort of thing themselves embody a religion: the very fervour of their opposition to 'traditional religion', or what they know of it, identifies them as devoted followers of a dream. I share their suspicion of many religious forms: that is the object of my present investigation – to find out what religion can be affirmed. 'Born-again atheism', so to call it, is one religious form, and not necessarily the worst.

So perhaps a kind of religious change should help us, a waking-up to an appalling loss, a realization that things matter to us in a way we only mouthed before. Such awakenings, like any addict's, will need careful guidance, lest we sleep again. We may stay awake awhile by glancing back at the thing that startled us, or chanting the appropriate slogans with clenched fists, or find some enemy to shout at, or lay down rules of behaviour for the times we know will come when we no longer feel like doing what we sleepily aver we should. These safeguards create new sects, and new sectarian wars: beliefs and rituals that, to outsiders, seem identical are the occasion of splenetic rage amongst the half-asleep.

But does our ecological crisis require a change? The alcoholic may need to be woken up to attempt the long and difficult recovery, but waking only shows her what was known, though notionally, before: that alcohol intoxicates. Waking to realize, and act on, the discovery that pollution knows no frontiers, that oil wells run dry, that famine, plague and war are on the way, what do we realize that we did not know before? Surely, mere self-interest will require us to act, or to call on our friends, as any addict might, to help us act.

The trouble is that our situation is not that of the solitary addict. However difficult it may be to make her problem real to herself, however difficult it may be to hold herself to what intelligence requires of her, yet she can be sure of consequences: if she manages not to drink, she won't get drunk. But even if I managed not to drive a car, my neighbours would. Even if my State stopped burning fossil fuels, the rest of the world would not. All that our individual action or inaction does is put us at a disadvantage as the world decays. Our ecological crisis is the product of many million individual decisions. Many of us may really believe that we are damaging the world, but carry on doing so because refraining does no good if no one else refrains, and if perchance they do, perhaps we needn't. To this familiar 'tragedy of the commons'[8] there may be a political or military solution. As individuals, corporations, nation-states we need to tell each other that 'we will stop polluting if you do so as well, and hereby authorize some global authority to hold us to the bargain, as long as you do too'. But my suspicion is that so final a surrender of personal and national sovereignty can only happen on the very edge of ruin, when it will be too late to save us anyway.

> There is only one rational way in which states coexisting with other states can emerge from the lawless condition of pure warfare. Just like individual men they must renounce their savage and lawless freedom, adapt themselves to public coercive laws, and thus form an international state (*civitas gentium*) which would necessarily continue to grow until it embraced all the peoples of the earth.[9]

But Kant himself added that no such union could be expected, and others (reasonably enough) have doubted that any such world-state would be worth honouring. I agree with those American 'anti-federalists' who opposed the American Union: 'The same government pervading a vast extent of territory terrifies the minds of individuals into meanness and submission. All human authority, however organized, must have confined limits, or insolence and oppression will prove the offspring of its grandeur, and the difficulty or rather impossibility of escape prevents resistance.'[10] My concern in these lectures is with a different sort of solution to the tragedy: what possible alteration in our motives and morale can save us from self-interested destruction of our vital interests? The answer, if there is one, would be relevant even to the political solution: civil peace, co-operation, sacrifice cannot long be enforced by the sword alone. We need to believe that the sword only enables us to do what we'd prefer.

So what alteration or new emphasis is needed, and must it be religious? Our tragedy is that we look to consequences: seeing that our actions will make no difference save to disadvantage us, we go on as we were, and all end where we'd rather not. If instead we did our acts 'as worship', not looking to the end, we'd act more sensibly. Even utilitarians can agree that better results may be obtained by people not wholly motivated by expectable utility. Those of us who are not utilitarians are bound to think that there are some things we could not or should not ever agree to be paid to do. 'How much would you take to eat your parents?', King Darius asked the Greeks. Religion, in this wide sense, is what ties us down, and gives us reason not to seize advantages, but rather sacrifice them. Born-again atheists, like other martyrs, will not pray, sing hymns or genuflect, even though (on their account) there is no god to punish them for blasphemy and many temporal advantages to conformity. A similarly religious environmentalist must reckon that her doing what wastes or destroys or poisons is still wrong even if there is strong reason to think that others will do it even if she does not. A people thus religious, on awakening to their predicament, have some chance of turning aside in time because each individual will reckon it right to turn even if perchance the others didn't. Religion, as the sense of absolutes, would be a thing good utilitarians would wish widely spread. What content such a worshipful mentality should have, what absolutes, are the questions I shall try to grapple with.

## C Pointing the finger

In 1967 Lynn White gave forceful expression to the common judgement that 'we shall continue to have a worsening ecological crisis until we reject the Christian axiom that nature has no reason for existence save to serve man'.[11] As long as we think that there are no proper limits on what we may individually and collectively do with the world wherein we find ourselves, we shall do what looks like bringing the best advantage. Even if, other things being equal, we would genuinely prefer to live among established woodlands and breathe clean air, we also have other wants, and know that other people have them too. What our religion lets us use, we will. So 'the Christian axiom', if such it is, gets in the way of crisis-resolution.

It is easy enough to devise an answer to what White suggested.[12] It certainly can't be *only* Christians that pollute the world. White himself acknowledged that the Pleistocene extinctions might well have been caused by human fire-drives. An American ecofeminist, by the way, is romantically inclined to speak of those animals' 'giving themselves for food':[13] so easy it is to think that our ancestors, not having been Christians, were guiltless. Robinson Jeffers, whose poetry will concern me later, had a harsher view, characterizing the burning alive of a trapped mammoth as an example of original sin.[14]

> As for me I would rather
> Be a worm in a wild apple than a son of man.
> But we are what we are, and we might remember
> Not to hate any person, for all are vicious;
> And not be astonished at any evil, all are deserved;
> And not to fear death; it is the only way to be cleansed.

Human beings hunted kinds to death by fire. Human beings, turning from such bloody acts to agriculture (perhaps because there were too few prey left to kill), drained the land of its fertility and seasoned it with salt. Human beings cut down forests and let the soil dry out and blow away. We did all this without being Christians, and in doing so behaved, most probably, like any successful species.

> The transformation of forests and grasslands into brambles and dustbowls has been going on for thousands of years. Ancient civilizations collapsed when they destroyed their agricultural base, but these were local problems. Now civilization is worldwide and if our worldwide resources in soil are further depleted, there will be nowhere left to turn.[15]

But though Christians cannot be exclusively to blame, and plenty of non-Christian countries have done as badly or still worse, it may still be true that 'the Christian axiom' prevents a resolution. The argument in the literature of environmentalism is not well conducted. The evidence for the existence of the axiom seems at times to consist of Ronald Reagan's throw-away remark that 'when you've seen one redwood tree you've seen them all', uncritical quotation of the biblical injunction to have 'dominion', and an equally uncritical conviction that Christianity, being dualist, anti-materialist, and founded on the idea of a transcendent, male deity, must be opposed to nature, animals and women. The speech attributed to Chief Seattle in 1854[16] (but mostly composed in 1970) pictures Christians as people utterly divorced from the material earth, expecting to walk with their transcendent God in some quite other world, and all too likely to regard this world as mere material (without being in the least ascetic in their use of it). Many commentators, by way of reply, have pointed out that biblical theists are usually powerfully convinced of the real and sacramental importance of the material universe. The God of the Bible – and also the Koran – is present in the world, and so far from licensing our exploitation of it, places limits on it with a threat of judgement. To that topic I shall be returning.

Nor is it any easier to convict mediaeval Christianity of any contempt for 'Mother Nature'. As Carolyn Merchant's study *The Death of Nature*[17] makes clear, the dominant morality of that time was opposed to mining in that it, literally, devastated land, and metaphorically or mystically raped the earth. When Callenbach's rather irritating Ecotopians remark 'Who would use an earth-mover on his own mother?'[18] they are reviving mediaeval rhetoric. That same rhetoric is commonly attributed to 'aboriginals' and 'native peoples': thus Warwick Fox quotes an Amerindian response to the offer of a more effective plough, 'shall I tear my mother's breast?'.[19] It is alarmingly easy to locate such notions amongst 'aboriginals'. As Merchant also says, that model was undermined by commercial needs that were long resisted by the Church authorities. Nor were those authorities merely 'spiritual'. On the contrary, as Boulding has observed, in the Benedictines 'for almost the first time in history we had intellectuals who worked with their hands, and belonged to a religion which regarded the physical world as in some sense sacred and capable of enshrining goodness'.[20] Doubtless those Benedictines acted in ways I might myself think wrong, but it is just not true that their creed licensed either literal or symbolic rape. Bahro may even be right to suspect that we need a new 'Benedictine' Order.[21]

The impulse to blame our situation on Christians, Hebrews, Greeks or, generally, patriarchs is one that most serious environmentalists would normally seek to curb. Selecting villains, and identifying ourselves with their historical victim, is just the sort of 'dualism' we should seek to avoid. Supposing that events have simple, linear causes is to forget how complex history is. Supposing that human beings do things because of their beliefs, and not because their material situation determines that result, is perhaps a little too idealist. These failings are compounded by romantic fantasies of some place far away or long ago when people lived in 'harmony with nature'. Perhaps they did, or do. But the suspicion, or my suspicion, must be that this was because they lacked the power to do much else.

'You want to leave things as they are and just take what you need. Don't be wasteful, that's what the elders taught': a Suquamish Indian named Martha George.[22] Sound advice, no doubt, but this is the voice of the poor throughout the ages. If it works, don't mend it. Make do, and mend. The limits within which our forebears worked were those of necessity. There are few known cases of a people who have deliberately stayed poor. Modern environmentalists may wish to insist, for example, that 'it is not *our* ecology, we are *its*', that we belong to the land that shaped us, that 'we are the rocks dancing'.[23] There is something to be said for this, as I shall suggest in a later chapter. But it is all too easy to reach back in our past or in our knowledge of contemporary custom to discover people who think of themselves like that, who say that they cannot sell the land or conceive of themselves away from it. The fact remains that people given the opportunity *do* leave the land (and we suddenly become astonishingly sympathetic to the elders who would stop the young from going). 'City air makes free', the proverb says, and thousands of our ancestors, escaping from serfdom as part of the land, were glad it did. We may now be confident that industrial civilization has its costs, that we need to recover some less bourgeois virtues. But let us not pretend that life on the land or on the sea was romantically suffused with meaning. Let us recall instead that even the horrors of Britain's Industrial Revolution were considered better than the life people left, and that another name for being 'one with the land' is serfdom. I admit that I am here ignoring certain other pressures, of usury and enclosure. But I doubt if even a less usurious, genuinely 'peasant economy' was without its trials. Fraser Harrison, commenting on George Clausen's 1896 picture of a boy scaring birds in March, remarks that

> here is a countryside no less brutalising, unhealthy (the boy will surely contract bronchitis) and indifferent to human needs and potential than the city's factories and slums. This child has been separated from his community and friends to perform a mechanical task in harsh conditions for negligible wages (which even so will add significantly to his family's income).[24]

So perhaps the successive changes in our history owe less to religious feeling or theological doctrine than to the ordinary need of people to make a better life somewhere. In our beginnings we had simply to endure the cycles of glut and shortage, gorging ourselves when we had the chance. When it became possible to store our surplus, we could avoid a sharp collapse, perhaps at the price,

Rabbinic thought suggests, of enslaving ourselves to the one who had secured the store.[25] The possibility of 'borrowing upon our expectations', either literally or in the extended sense of deferring the environmental problems we create, creates still greater reserves. The possibility of living off a seemingly inexhaustible capital, of fossil fuels and minerals, releases our imagination, until we stand upon a high plateau from which we must either fall, or fly into the empyrean. At each stage of our history people made what seemed to them good choices: that the bills are falling due does not make our forebears fools or knaves.

## D Enlightenment axioms?

They were not fools, maybe, nor can we sensibly blame 'the Christians', 'the Europeans', the military–industrial complex or the man in the moon. Nor is Christian doctrine wholly inhospitable even to the very 'deepest' of ecological concerns. But it is still worth asking if there are assumptions, adopted for whatever reason, that get in our way. In Wendell Berry's words

> I believe that until fairly recently our destructions of nature were more or less unwitting – the by-products, so to speak, of our ignorance or weakness or depravity. It is our present principled and elaborately rationalised rape and plunder of the natural world that is a new thing under the sun.[26]

If people think, or feel, that the world is made 'for them', or that there is nothing valuable but people, or that only rational order, imposed from without, makes chaos bearable, or that the rational intellect forbids emotional involvement in the lower orders, or that the material world is what we must abandon, they may not be restrained from actions liable to have bad consequences, even if they think those consequences bad. If those are the actual axioms of folk-Christianity perhaps we do need a new religion. It would be absurd to blame Aristotle for the existence of slavery, an institution that long outlasted and preceded him, but it may still be important to refute the Aristotelian arguments that slave-owners sometimes used, even if we know that they would willingly use any arguments, and never showed any sign of accepting Aristotle's other, and more deeply felt, beliefs.[27] It is correspondingly important for environmentalists to deflate such reasons as are offered for not minding much about the situation, and for Christians, if they do care, to show their Christianity is not an obstacle.

So far I have suggested that something like a religion is required. If there is indeed a crisis, as I think, we shall not cope with it unless we are woken to a real assent, unless we can do our acts 'as worship' without hope or fear of consequences, unless we can recognize a 'sacred' limit on our actions, unless these features are or could be widely shared in the world community. One of the many problems is that even if we prove to need a 'new religion', a new religion is a thing we emphatically don't need. The crisis would be far worse if wars of religion spread – a point on which I agree with born-again atheists, while noting that they do not notice that their own conviction is just such another begetter of holy wars. We need a radical change of life which yet, somehow, confirms and can be endorsed by all the old religions. I don't say this is possible.

But must it not be ruled out from the start? All the great religions, except perhaps Hinduism, distinguish between persons and the parts they play; none would agree that people are merely part of nature. All of them, except perhaps Hinduism, think that people must be the first concern of people; none of them would pay more than lip-service to the idea that humankind is not the last, best effort of whatever makes the world. Humanism, briefly, is a significant strand in all the great religions: that is why they are called 'great'. Humanists of whatever style require us to believe in individuals, in individual human worth, in the reliability of human reason and the hope of progress. I shall have more to say of humanism in later chapters. In this I wish to concentrate on one feature attributed to humanism, and certainly often present in the great religions, namely its dichotomizing tendency.

Long ago or far away, romantics tell us, people were unselfconsciously united with their world. Nineteenth-century romantics liked to think 'the Greeks' were like that; late twentieth-century ones locate the fantasy in Old Europe or amongst native Americans.[28] People did not think of themselves as independent individuals, but as members of a shining congregation of gods, spirits, dryad-infested trees and families. They did not distinguish culture or art or custom from natural happenings. They did not imagine an 'objective world' behind or apart from the world experienced by them. They had no reason to distinguish thought and matter, *res cogitans* and *res extensa*, nor did they think that the truth was to be discovered by a resolute attention to physical geometry. The real world and the world of our experience were one, and to know it better was to know its values. Nothing was available to us as mere material, for everything was present to us with its proper value. The names of things dictated what their values and their natures were. They did not so much 'live in harmony with nature', as reckon 'natural' only what harmonized with their natures. That archaic unity was broken by the dichotomizing intellect, and our spiritual crisis is mirrored in the ecological.

There is, perhaps, some truth in this. We have constructed our idea of the 'real world', the world as it is apart from sentient and human experience, by a careful inattention to what usually matters most to us. Moral and aesthetic values as well as secondary qualities, historical associations and, in the end, identities are functions of our involvement in the world: the truth of things is modelled by detachment, non-involvement. Having decided that no really true proposition can have moral implications, we are disingenuously surprised to realize that moral propositions can't be true, that values can only be projections of our values, as dryads are only representations of an older imaginative involvement in the world of trees. Because our idea of the real world is of a world without values, we conclude that the real world has no value, that it is available for any use we please. ' "It's only electricity" implies that electricity as belonging to the natural order is no more than a thing to be manipulated by man.'[29]

Some commentators have responded by insisting on the primacy and inescapability of the life-world, the undivided world of experience. The world of physical geometry, by this account, is not the causal origin of experience: it has, after all, been defined as a world without *qualia* and therefore provides no intelligible explanation of their existence. It is often beautiful, precisely because we have constructed it to suit our ideas of beauty. It often has a certain usefulness: to predict the path of a projectile we need only study the geometry, and not its colour, aesthetic values or familiar name. The conviction that geometry will one day help us to explain human or animal behaviour is as blind and unreasonable a faith as any. Ordinarily academic anti-realists (which is to say: philosophers who have come to doubt that it even makes sense to suppose that we could uncover a reality that was not *our* reality) rarely draw the obvious conclusion that dryads are, after all, 'real' or 'quasi-real' inhabitants of the human world, not to be denied existence in favour of mere lumber. Nor do they explain how they can continue to pay lip-service to the notion that the world existed for many thousand million years before human or sentient experience. Fantasy is what Enlightenment thinkers once opposed, in the name of the 'true philosophy'. Consider Thomas Sprat:[30]

> The poets of old to make all things look more venerable than they were, devised a thousand false Chimaeras; on every Field, River, Grove and Cave they bestowed a Fantasm of their own making: With these they amazed the world. . . . And in the modern Ages these Fantastical Forms were reviv'd and possessed Christendom. . . . All which abuses if those acute Philosophers did not promote, yet they were never able to overcome; nay, not even so much as King Oberon and his invisible Army. But from the time in which the Real Philosophy has appear'd there is scarce any whisper remaining of such horrors. . . . The course of things goes quietly along, in its own true channel of Natural Causes and Effects. For this we are beholden to Experiments; which though they have not yet completed the discovery of the true world, yet they have already vanquished those wild inhabitants of the false world, that us'd to astonish the minds of men.

Romantics of a less conventional kind do draw something like the obvious conclusions, and often with an eye to the environmental consequences. Perhaps we would treat the land better if we allowed ourselves to be conscious of it as a land suffused with memories, symbolism, values. Considered geometrically, a hill, a lake, a spinney is one shape out of many, with no particular call on our attention. It may still have a claim on us when considered as an historical entity, the name of remembered ancestors and earth-spirits. Instead of geometry, geomancy.

The land is a mnemonic. By this I mean, at its crudest, that we are reminded of personal, tribal memories by features of the landscape, whether 'built' or 'natural'. Those memories are living realities for us, confronting us when we confront the landmarks. They are what our forebears called dead heroes, spirits, godlets, and are (for all of us) as real as the images and meanings we convey through literal texts like this one. Those who would burn books do not burn merely paper: they (foolishly, no doubt) attempt to destroy spirits. Those who remodel landscapes do the like, most often to fill them up again with *their* own spirits. The kind of religious enterprise described by would-be Celts or Native Americans (sometimes, it must be feared, without much respect for people who actually are Native Americans or Celts or what you will) takes these spirits seriously. If we meditate upon imagined landmarks (whether these be ancient trees, or battle sites, or large-scale fictions like the zodiacal figures around Glastonbury Tor[31]) we will find our old self stretched and changed to accommodate the godlets. Maybe (who knows) such imagined figures are more than helpful fictions. It is certainly true that make-believe like this facilitates the construction of new arguments, helps us to see things differently: it is standard advice indeed to sufferers from writers' block to pretend that someone else, from deep within, is writing.[32] Some 'New Age' writers have apparently convinced themselves that they can be the mediums for godlets that exist beyond, as well as in, their own imagining. Those who imagine what the land, the tree, the stream would say, perhaps succeed in hearing what it does.

But although the attempt to resurrect or slip back into the old world may be well-intentioned, I am doubtful that it serves the environmental needs. Many of the gods and godlets people have imagined have been demons, and those crude missionaries who took it on themselves to cut down sacred groves may have had a point. If the grove were gone, the memory might fade, and have less influence in the waking day. Maybe Chesterton was right, that the past had to be purged and purified. Gardens, woods and the stars themselves were polluted (that is, the world of nature as it features in our imaginative experience was polluted) by the perversions of late paganism.[33] Only when four centuries of ascetic practice had purified the imagination could St Francis rededicate the natural world. 'Man has stripped from his soul the last rag of nature-worship, and can return to nature.'[34] Those are not the only possible corruptions. There have been many life-worlds, after all, and some of them have identified the creatures with whom we share the land as walking larders, prey, vermin, pets. Returning to an innocent, unselfconscious identification with the world in which we find ourselves would be to surround ourselves with loyal dogs, proud peacocks, horridly half-human apes, self-sacrificial lambs, and human beings themselves identified by their social roles and imagined histories. It was no small achievement to discover that people, animals, the land have their own being outside the names we put on them. It would be no advance at all to forego our real engagement with a really Other being: it would, instead of waking up, be sinking back to sleep.

Accustomed language governs thought: what is needed is the sudden realization of something that transcends such custom.

> In nothing is the modern German more modern, or more mad, than in his dream of finding a German word for everything; eating his language, or in other words biting his tongue. And in nothing were the mediaevals more free and sane than in their acceptance of names and emblems from outside their most beloved limits.[35]

The sense of a reality transcending and supporting all our little worlds is seldom far away in Chesterton's writings, and I shall have more to say of it hereafter.

> There is at the back of all our lives an abyss of light, more blinding and unfathomable than any abyss of darkness; and it is the abyss of actuality, of existence, of the fact that things truly are, and that we ourselves are incredibly and sometimes almost incredulously real. It is the fundamental fact of being, as against not being; it is unthinkable, yet we cannot unthink it, though we may sometimes be unthinking about it; unthinking and especially unthanking. For he who has realized this reality knows that it does outweigh, literally to infinity, all lesser regrets or arguments for negation, and that under all our grumblings there is a subconscious substance of gratitude.[36]

'I would maintain', he had said fifteen years before, 'that thanks are the highest form of thought.'[37] Heidegger made a similar association of thought and thanksgiving, a similar contrast between Being and *Dasein*, though he also spent much of his energy in finding German words for everything. He failed to discern the danger in either enterprise.

Despite the rhetoric of romantics, there is little evidence that 'spirit-haunted glades' are treated better than mere timber: the spirits that haunt them, after all, are created by our needs and imagination, and perhaps especially by our need to evade guilt. There is little enough to choose between the butcher who thinks the animal is meat, and the priest who thinks it goes consenting to its death: maybe the sacrificial beast is allowed a little dignity, but it still ends in pieces. Those Christian environmentalists who, from a different metaphysical background, speak of man (*sic*) as 'the world's high priest' should likewise remember what priests, in Greece and Israel, actually did.[38]

Wakening to a religion of romance and ritual is unlikely to help. If the only reality we need consider is the life-world of our innocent experience, we may as well solve the crisis by calling it something different. Pollution and environmental degradation are no more than evolution in action, or artistic restructurings of a former world. Romantic ecofeminists of a kind that I shall describe in my next chapter, will sometimes admit that stories about peace-loving Neolithic matriarchies, 'in harmony with nature', with undichotomized life-worlds, are not historical, but only helpful fables. They may add that academic histories are no more. But in that case we can as easily invent a past to evade the pain of loss. Big Brother, in Orwell's

*1984*, need only claim to have *raised* the chocolate ration instead of lowering it for this to be 'true'. If what's 'true' is what the Party said, we need fear no crisis from external nature. But it is just that willed evasion of real consequences that has been our curse. Kipling's characterization of those who 'rose to suppose themselves kings over all things created – to decree a new earth at a birth without labour or sorrow' applies as well to romantics as to technophiles.

> They denied what they dared not abide if it came to the trial;
> But the sword that was forged while they lied did not heed their denial.[39]

We cannot and must not retreat to an imagined innocence when we did not distinguish between our fables and reality. But neither need we accept a pure objectivism, defining the 'real' world as what does not matter. The then Nigerian Minister of Agriculture announced, in 1982, that his ministry had abandoned 'Western scientific definitions of drought which depended on measuring quantities of rainfall', and adopted another: 'not as much water as the people need.'[40] He had a point. Pure objectivism was always silly: if no true proposition carries any moral implication then no true proposition ought to be believed. The contemplation of truth, through the recognition of a kind of beauty, is a duty only if there are such duties; if there aren't we can have no notion of a truth we should not deny. When we wake up to a real assent, to a deep recognition of real existences outwith the purposes we dreamily endorsed for them, we are in the same instant recognizing something worthy of respect. Physical geometry reveals a truth, and so do other disciplines. Romantics who rightly reject the fable that reality is only geometric but fall back on geomancy are guilty of exactly those false dichotomies that bring the rational realist into disrepute.

So what are the roots of our crisis, and what spiritual changes do we need to cope with them? By my account the crisis is the unintended outcome of a general wish to live a little better. 'The better you live, the more oil you use', according to the Exxon advertisement. We have devised all manner of excuses for not troubling ourselves too much about what we do. We pretend that animals give themselves, or are given to us, or are merely meat or matter in motion. We pretend that the airs and waters are indefatigably purifying, that the land need not lie fallow, that Nature or the Lord will surely keep us going because we are so nice. We don't act as we do because we believe these things, but believe, or pretend to believe them, because we want to go on acting just like that. If we are to have any chance of stopping, we must wake up to a real appreciation of a genuine Otherness, a world not limited by what we make of it. So far from giving up rational realism and the dichotomizing intellect we must exert our intellectual powers, must make distinctions, must seek to see things as they are, whether we will or no.

Then what is the answer? Not to be deluded by dreams,
To know that great civilizations have broken down into violence, and their tyrants
    come, many times before.
When open violence appears, to avoid it with honor or choose the least ugly
    faction; the evils are essential.
To keep one's integrity, be merciful and uncorrupted and not wish for evil; and not
    be duped
By dreams of universal justice and happiness. These dreams will not be fulfilled.
To know this, and know that however ugly the parts appear the whole remains
    beautiful. A severed hand
Is an ugly thing, and man dissevered from the earth and stars and his history . . .
    for contemplation or in fact . . .
Often appears atrociously ugly. Integrity is wholeness, the great beauty is
Organic wholeness, the wholeness of life and things, the divine beauty of the
    universe. Love that, not man
Apart from that, or else you will share man's pitiful confusions, or drown in
    despair when his days darken.[41]

## Notes

1. A. Toynbee and D. Ikeda, *Choose Life* (Oxford University Press: London, 1976), p. 324.

2. W. Blake, 'Marriage of Heaven and Hell', §9 in *Complete Writings*, ed. G. Keynes (Clarendon Press: Oxford, 1966), p. 152 (my italics).

3. A term of art to class together the great 'religions of the Book' (at least Judaism, Christianity and Islam) as other religious groups are classed together as Hindu or Buddhist: see *The Mysteries of Religion* (Blackwell: Oxford, 1986). I do not mean to imply that all religions of the Book agree, even on essentials – any more than all 'Buddhists' (a group including radically diverse sects and philosophies: Theravada, Mahayana, Madhyamika) do.

4. G. K. Chesterton, *Collected Poems* (Methuen: London, 1950), p. 326.

5. Margaret Thatcher, 27 September 1988; cited by D. Pearce, A. Markandya and E. B. Barbier, *Blueprint for a Green Economy* (Earthscan Publications: London, 1989), p. 27.

6. See my *Civil Peace and Sacred Order* (Clarendon Press: Oxford, 1989).

7. Addiction is 'any process . . . which takes control of us, causing us to do and think things that are inconsistent with our personal values and leading us to become progressively more compulsive and obsessive': Anne Wilson Schoef, *When Society Becomes an Addict* (Harper & Row: New York, 1987); cited by Matthew Fox, *Creation Spirituality* (Harper: San Francisco, 1991), p. 82.

8. G. Hardin, 'The tragedy of the commons', *Science* 162 (1968), pp. 1243–8.

9. I. Kant, 'Perpetual peace', *Kant's Political Writings*, ed. H. Reiss (Cambridge: Cambridge University Press, 1970), p. 105.

10. (1788): M. Borden (ed.), *The Anti-Federalist Papers* (Michigan State University Press: Ann Arbor, 1965), p. 8.

11. L. White, 'The roots of our ecologic crisis', *Science* 155 (1967), pp. 1203–7.

12. See J. Barr, 'Man and Nature: the ecological controversy and the Old Testament', *Bulletin of John Rylands Library* 55 (1972), pp. 9–32.

13. Starhawk, *The Spiral Dance* (Harper & Row: New York, 1984, 10th edn), p. 17.

14. R. Jeffers, 'Original Sin' in *The Double Axe and Other Poems* (Liveright: New York, 1977), pp. 145–6.

15. John B. Cobb, *Is It Too Late? A Theology of Ecology* (Bruce: Beverly Hills, 1972), p. 4.

16. John Seed, Pat Fleming, Joanna Macy and Arne Naess, *Thinking Like a Mountain: Towards a Council of All Beings* (Heretic Books: London, 1988), pp. 67–73. See J. B. Callicott, *In Defense of the Land Ethic* (State University of New York Press: Albany, 1989), p. 204.

17. Carolyn Merchant, *The Death of Nature* (Wildwood House: London, 1982), pp. 29ff.

18. E. Callenbach, *Ecotopia* (Pluto Press: London, 1978), p. 29: a fairly conventional post-Morris utopia.

19. W. Fox, *Approaching Deep Ecology* (University of Tasmania Press, 1986), p. 76: cited by A. Dobson, *Green Political Thought* (Unwin Hyman: London, 1990), p. 59.

20. R. Foricy, *Wind and Sea Obey Him* (SCM: London, 1982), p. 75, quoting K. R. Boulding, *Meaning of the Twentieth Century* (Harper & Row: New York, 1964), p. 6.

21. R. Bahro, *Building the Green Movement* (GMP: London, 1986), p. 90.

22. *The Eyes of Chief Seattle* (Suquamish Museum: Seattle), p. 30.

23. John Seed in *Thinking Like a Mountain*, p. 36.

24. Fraser Harrison, *Strange Land* (Sidgwick & Jackson: London, 1982), p. 96.

25. Joseph, in this interpretation, is the villain, who sold the Egyptian people into slavery to Pharaoh, and whose own people paid the price of it.

26. W. Berry, *What Are People For?* (Rider Books: London, 1990), p. 108.

27. See A. Pagden, *The Fall of Natural Man* (Cambridge University Press: Cambridge, 1982).

28. See E. Craig, *The Mind of God and the Works of Man* (Clarendon Press: Oxford, 1987).

29. A. D. Galloway, *The Cosmic Christ* (Nisbet & Co: London, 1951), p. 33.

30. Thomas Sprat, *History of the Royal Society* (1702), p. 340; cited by B. Willey, *The Seventeenth Century Background* (Hutchinson: London, 1934), p. 213.

31. 'Fictions', because they almost certainly weren't there until, quite recently, people began imagining they saw them.

32. See L. Hudson, *Frames of Mind* (Penguin: Harmondsworth, 1970), pp. 86ff.

33. G. K. Chesterton, *St Francis of Assisi* (Hodder & Stoughton: London, 1923), pp. 29ff.

34. Chesterton, ibid., p. 39.

35. G. K. Chesterton, *Short History of England* (Chatto & Windus: London, 1917), p. 59.

36. G. K. Chesterton, *St Thomas Aquinas* (Hodder & Stoughton: London, 1933), p. 36.

37. Chesterton, *Short History*, p. 59.

38. See W. Burkert, *Homo Necans* (University of California: Berkeley, 1983).

39. R. Kipling, 'The City of Brass' in *Verse 1885–1926* (Hodder & Stoughton: London, 1927), pp. 313ff.

40. A. Wijkman and L. Timberlake, *Natural Disasters: Acts of God or Acts of Man* (Earthscan: London, 1984), p. 33.

41. R. Jeffers, 'The Answer' in *Selected Poetry* (Random House: New York, 1933), p. 594.

# The return of the Goddess

·····································

## A Further dangers of make-believe

I have suggested that, if we are to cope with our crisis, we must wake up to a real recognition of the world as something other than our obedient shadow, something or some things that we must recognize as sacred. We must both recognize the World as other than the human world, and recognize ourselves as inextricably dependent on that world. It is both our Other and our Origin, something unconstrained by our projected values and recognized as something by which we should be constrained. 'Honour your father and your mother that your days may be long in the land the Lord your God has given you': honour, in fact, the land, which is to say the complexity of earth, air and water and their living denizens. This recognition of the Other as something which we should respect exactly as *not* being ourselves, nor even very much like ourselves, is recognized by Murdoch (in the Anglophone tradition) and by Levinas (in the 'Continental').[1] This is what makes some recent moral argument rather suspect. Moralists have tended to suggest that it is in so far as things are like 'us' that they are deserving of respect: but the better way is to respect them as *not* being like ourselves, and so to allow them to *be*. But even if this view were challenged it is vital to remember that, *pace* Metz, Rorty, Derrida or postmodern ecofeminists, the world emphatically *does* 'exist in itself over against human beings'.[2] Of course it is also true that, in so far as we are aware of the world at all, it becomes part of the story we tell. Of course, since we are utterly dependent on the world (and so a minor part of it) there can be no gap between Us and It. But what It is does not depend on what we say it is. All attempts to evade this fact, like similar attempts to evade the laws of logic, seem to me appallingly misguided. I am especially distressed by would-be feminists who pursue that path, and claim that notions like truth, or fact, or logical validity are male inventions. It is a fact that women have been and are oppressed and vilified: it is no answer at all to say there are no facts, no laws of evidence. To agree that women are bad at logical argument and should be proud of it is as inept a response to slander as to agree that women are bad drivers: the rules of the road, I suppose, are male inventions, and real women should therefore drive with passion and intuitive élan. Anti-realism, anti-rationalism are absurd and dangerous responses to the misuse of reason and realism. Women, as a class, are *not* bad drivers, nor are they bad logicians.

The obvious and widely recognized image of the living world, our origin, is the Earth Mother. How literal that label is can be obscure. Even those who seriously profess to worship the Goddess are careful to speak in decently non-literal ways. Thus Starhawk, the ecofeminist and self-styled witch I mentioned in the last chapter:

> When I say Goddess I am not talking about a being somewhere outside of this world nor am I proposing a new belief system. I am talking about choosing an attitude: choosing to take this living world, the people and creatures in it, as the ultimate meaning and purpose of life, to see the world, the earth and our lives as sacred.[3]

I remark in passing that Starhawk here implicitly accepts a false dichotomy between talking of Deity as one being among many (like a celestial Yeti) and reinterpreting such God-or-Goddess-talk as merely expressive of an 'attitude', a blik.[4] Her implication seems to be that the living world does not demand our recognition, but that we choose to respect it. Its 'sacredness' is only a projection of our unfettered choice – but it is difficult to see that such choices have much power. What has no value over and above my choice has none at all.[5] As Merchant observes, the living earth our mother whom mediaeval moralists feared to ravage or disembowel became an obvious and easy target when commercial needs grew stronger.[6]

Really, I think, Starhawk and others mean to recognize the living world as sacred, and think that those who disagree are wrong. I suspect that secretly they really believe that this sacred world is such as to communicate both energy and understanding to its devotees, that it is indeed the Goddess. If that is so then Goddess-worship is a candidate for the kind of awakening we need. I confess that I have my doubts. I wish that devotees did not say things like this: 'Nouns are patriarchal. They separate us from things, naming the thing and making it an object. American Indian languages have no nouns, only relationships.'[7] Or this: 'Anthropocentrism is a peculiarly male sin.'[8] I wish that reports from communes, covens and Goddess-oriented communities did not reveal so much of malice, power-seeking and intolerable folly of the kind that longer-established churches recognize and seek to repel.[9] I wish that ecofeminists did not so readily believe, and refuse to reconsider, fables of Neolithic matriarchies or ersatz 'Old Religions' coined from the books of Margaret Murray or Robert Graves. I wish that they did not so readily equate the Enlightenment with Bacon and Gassendi – apparently unaware that just about all the great seventeenth- and eighteenth-century philosophers *rejected* atomism, individualism and subjective moralism. I wish that they did not so readily seize on scientific hypotheses they chance to like (like 'woman's aquatic origins', or Lovelock's Gaia) and turn them into myths. We need a new religion, maybe, but we also desperately need an eye for evidence.

Are my objections to the point? Does not any new religion, and even any new scientific paradigm, make new things sound quite plausible long before they are proved? Any new idea has its own resonance, and many of the lesser ideas it spawns will prove in the end mistaken even if the central idea is sound. Disciples of the new idea are wise not to dismiss those sub-ideas on the word of those devoted to an older paradigm. The stories of horrific child-abuse that Freudians thought were evidence of endogenous traumas turn out, to a later generation, to be evidence, exactly, of horrific child-abuse. Freud, in the event, would have been wiser to accept his first understanding even when, by the canons of patriarchal law, it could not be proved. Maybe many seemingly random claims of modern ecofeminists will turn out true as well: the figure of nine million dead in the post-Reformation witch-hunts, seemingly invented from thin air in 1951 and devotedly repeated since, *may* turn out truer than the forty to sixty thousand, 'distinguished only by the fact that they had made enemies',[10] proposed by more conventional scholars.

It may be so, but I can only repeat my intuition that such Goddess-worship neither will nor should have much success until it takes the laws of evidence more seriously. At the moment most of their insights, real or otherwise, are borrowed from more conventional scholars or from obvious and admitted poets like Graves. Margaret Murray's books, for example, 'had the curious status of an orthodoxy which was believed by everybody except those who happened to be experts in the subject'.[11] The supposed evidence for Neolithic matriarchies was similarly demolished back in 1969.[12] That Amerindians lived 'in harmony with nature' continues to be asserted despite the blatant differences between such 'Amerindians' across the continent (as well talk about Eurasians), and despite the archaeological evidence of massive buffalo drives, and the anthropological of casual cruelty. Much of this is the same romanticism as imagines that 'the countryside' is more 'natural' than the city: even wilderness areas are made by people; even cities are part of creation – as Matthew Fox recognizes.[13] If the Goddess is a real revelation its worshippers need fear no real truths, and should be prepared to risk their own ideas.

But as Aristotle showed us long ago, and Blake confirmed, there is a truth in every serious idea. I see no reason to doubt the genuinely religious feeling of some Goddess-worshippers, and reckon the emergence of the Goddess as a religious archetype even amongst the more conventionally religious an event of some significance. The question is: is this the proper way to go, whatever the extravagances of some devotees?

## B The living world

I wish to consider first the notion of the world as a single, living whole; second, the possibility of participatory knowledge; third, the propriety of female metaphors; and fourth, the kind of limits on our action that such a Goddess sets. Some of what I have to say will be of relevance to more than ecofeminists; some issues may not be resolved, if ever, till a later chapter.

First, that the world is a single living whole. In fact, what seems to be intended here is that the earth is such a whole. The whole world, after all, has been reckoned infinite since Giordano Bruno intuited the implications of Copernicus' theory – though there are actually good reasons to doubt that the material world is actually infinite.[14] Whether the world, the totality of all finite beings within a possibly infinite web of relationships, is a 'whole' at all, is moot. For all we know there may be infinitely many separate, almost-separate, spheres, and even if there aren't it is clear that we have no conception of 'the world' as a whole. And to anticipate a later point, there seems no way of telling when the totality is well or badly off. So our attention must be directed to the whole earth – except that the earth could no more stand alone than any of us could. If we do not exist as entities, as Lewis Thomas says,[15] because we are made up of pieces that 'we' don't control and cannot stand alone without the help of the corporeal universe, then neither is the earth an entity. The only real entity is God, as Descartes, despite his reputation for considering us atomic individuals divided from the world, declared.

But though neither the world 'as a whole' nor yet the earth can be conceived as one self-subsistent whole, there may still be an advantage in considering the earth as, relatively, whole. The icon of the earth seen from orbit certainly encourages that notion: it is so obviously a single bubble of life within a larger world, transforming solar energy into such complexity of living organism. It is quite understandable that this icon has played a part in diminishing political antagonism: we have one world only, and it is vulnerable. I do not mean that it is fragile: on the contrary, as Lovelock has pointed out, it is fortunately very tough indeed. That it looks like a whole is true: connections within the earth are manifold, connections across the permeable boundary are relatively simple, consisting mainly of radiant energy and cosmic dust. There are exchanges across the boundary, as there are also exchanges across the boundary of our skin. Deep ecologists remark upon the latter exchanges to remind us how much a part of the earth's life we are, as the earth is part of the cosmos. But we are still relatively separate entities, and so is the earth.

I pause to remark that dedicated anti-realists can of course deny that the stars are anything but flickers on mammalian retinas, or anecdotes about the far away. F. P. Ramsey remarked that he 'didn't really believe in astronomy, except as a complicated description of part of the course of human and possibly animal sensation'.[16] Genuine anti-realists might even doubt that such a description could be given. For them the life-world, easily equated with the earth, is not a whole for another reason: it cannot be grasped as a whole by anyone, since everything that is must be 'inside' it. But I am not now dealing with such fantasies.

So the earth looks like, and relatively speaking is, a single entity with manifold internal connections and relatively simple external ones. It is quite like a living cell, with a semi-permeable membrane to protect its varied innards from too great interference from or diffusion into the rest of the world.[17] Is it like a cell in any stronger sense, of somehow regulating what passes through its membrane and how its interior denizens react to each other? Lovelock's Gaia hypothesis is that it is.[18] In its origins this thesis is a simple and profoundly plausible one. Any living organism survives by keeping its environment within that range (of temperature or biochemical condition) wherein it flourishes. The bacterial organisms in particular, on which our life is founded, will seek to control their environment, and all successful life-forms since will both adapt to that fundamental milieu and add their own delicate adjustments. The net result is a world of interlocking engineers who keep global temperature, and global chemistry, far away from what they would be without living organisms and within a narrow range of possibilities. Lovelock has suggested that as solar temperature rises we may be nearing the limit of the capacity of existing systems to slow down global warming. The additional influence of human beings on so-called greenhouse gases may be too much, and the versatile bacteria have to adjust to a new norm far beyond what we ourselves could cope with. He has also, perhaps, provided evidence for a long-standing intuition that more complex, more diverse ecosystems are in some way 'stabler', and thereby offered an argument against allowing too many species extinctions.

This is more than a cute idea. Lovelock's evidence for the efficacy of these biological processes in preserving the living earth is that no alternative mechanism seems to work. The Earth has been held away from chemical equilibrium: by comparison with our near neighbours, the Earth's atmosphere has far more free oxygen, far more free nitrogen, than it would have had were there no living things to make that difference. Yet more puzzlingly, the proportion of free oxygen has remained stable ever since the gas was released in the world's first major 'pollution incident'. If the proportion of oxygen were to rise or fall beyond definite limits our kind of life would have perished. Obviously, since we are here, it hasn't done – but that is not an explanation. Problems increase: if the sun's temperature has been steadily rising (as astrophysical theory informs us), why hasn't the Earth's? If minerals have been being washed down into the sea, since first there were seas, why isn't the sea now far too salt for any living thing? It seems that it would only take sixty million years for the sea to reach the limit of what any organism can endure (after that osmotic pressure destroys the cells).

These problems – and Lovelock elaborates several others – have something of the same effect as Olbers' Paradox or Kelvin's Puzzle. In the last century Lord Kelvin pointed out that Darwinian evolution simply took too long, if the sun was burning in anything like the ways then known: it must have been so much hotter a thousand million years ago as to have burnt up our ancestors. Olbers pointed out that if the universe were infinite and homogenous there would be a star visible at every point of the night sky – and the sky would be ablaze with light. Kelvin meant, no doubt, to refute Darwin, but his puzzle was only resolved by the discovery of radioactive decay as a source of energy. Olbers did not suppose that he had proved night-time an illusion, but the paradox was only resolved by postulating that the material universe was finite. Lovelock's concatenated puzzles amount to this: how can our lifeline have survived when it requires so narrow a range of physical and chemical conditions which are always likely to be altered (by living things, or by external changes)? Obviously it has survived: but that is no more a sensible explanation than would be the suggestion that a prisoner whose life was dependent on the daily toss of a coin (heads she dies; tails she lives another day) need not be puzzled if she survives for fifty years. The Earth's temperature should have been steadily increasing; the sea's salinity should long ago have been as toxic as that of the Dead Sea; oxygen should have poured out till the globe was irrepressibly aflame, all life extinguished and oxygen-production suppressed; water should have been dissociated into hydrogen and oxygen, the oxygen tied down in oxides and the hydrogen escaped from the upper atmosphere. The survival of the living Earth is a standing miracle.

As a working scientist Lovelock has no inclination to believe in miracles, in the sense of willed interventions by an alien intelligence – any more than most of the great theistic philosophers have relished Newton's desperate suggestion that the hand of God was needed to preserve the solar system. Instead he proposed that living things, which created some of the problems, also worked to solve them. Briefly, there is a complex system of feedback mechanisms that together maintain the proper conditions for life, very much as any single organism maintains its own more-or-less stability in the exchange of materials. The living Earth was a homeostatic (or rather, in Waddington's phrase, a homeorhetic) system rather like such a living organism.

Lovelock also follows Lynn Margulis, one of his most eminent collaborators, in emphasizing the problems posed by eukaryotic cells and multi-cellular organisms (as well as hives and societies) for a sheerly competitive theory of evolutionary change. Eukaryotes have incorporated sometime independent entities as endosymbionts: instead of all-out war different entities co-operate in sustaining a larger whole. Chloroplasts descended from Archaean cyanobacteria power cabbages and redwood trees; our own cells require the constant co-operation of sometime alien organisms with their own genetic lifeline. As a larger whole is formed destructive competition at a lower level is restricted; or, putting it differently, every individual contributor to the next generation's gene-pool can increase its own 'genetic fitness' by co-operation (and has good reason to enforce such co-operation upon others). The Eighties ideology of individualist competition – fuelled even against their personal intentions by writers like Dawkins and Wilson[19] – needs to be severely modified to acknowledge the real abiding force of mutual aid, and the real organisms that arise from that co-operation.

Mainstream biologists are usually dismissive of 'Gaia': 'a metaphor, not a mechanism', according to Steven J. Gould,[20] or (yet more contemptuously) a surrender to the 'BBC Documentary Syndrome', whereby all is for the best in the best of all possible worlds (as Richard Dawkins asserts). Quite why the hypothesis has been dismissed so eagerly is not wholly clear. 'A metaphor': but so also is 'natural selection', and 'mechanism'. 'An excuse for thinking all is for the best': but Lovelock expressly and repeatedly emphasizes that the feed-back mechanisms he postulates are not directed at *our* survival, nor consciously directed at all, and that the teleological account he gives (as that the output of dimethyl sulphide by marine algae plays a major role in the transport of sulphur from the sea to the land, and so in the maintenance of land-life) rests upon a straightforwardly biochemical study of the mechanisms involved. The question is, what regulates that production, and would we have noticed it at all without having sought to find out how land-life can have got the sulphur that it needs? Plants do not photosynthesize 'to produce oxygen for us' (in Dawkins' mocking summary), but the whole system is now as dependent on their doing so as ever our personal survival is on the regulated production of our necessary hormones.

This Gaia hypothesis is a fascinating and quite plausible suggestion. Despite the hasty scorn heaped on it by conventional biologists at its first airing it conflicts with no known evolutionary principle.

Just as a cell's conduct can, in principle, be understood as the result of the reactions of all its parts, so also Gaia's. Gaia is just the total, interconnected, historically accidental process whereby bacteria and their parasites (that is, us) maintain things as they need them. Without such a process there can be no living things: no little enclaves on Mars, for example, unable to control their planetary environment. The Gaia hypothesis need make no great difference to the present biological paradigm – except to draw attention once again to the preponderance of co-operative over merely competitive organisms, a preponderance neglected by proponents of 'selfishness' as the sole driving force of evolutionary change. The Gaia hypothesis, any sensible biologist should admit, may well be true. But for that very reason it may not have the implications some environmentalists, including myself, have seen in it.[21]

First of all, there is no real need to consider Gaia to be a single organism, and Lovelock does occasionally regret the fact that he capitalized 'gaia'. The processes that variously maintain a world well suited first to bacterial and then to other, parasitic forms of life have no single governing principle, nor is there any vital centre of the living earth. Nor is there any need to think that those processes display intelligence in any sense requiring sentience or foresight. It is a significantly new emphasis in evolutionary theory to recall that life can change the environment as well as vice versa, and to emphasize co-operation more than competition. But there is no *scientific* basis for the suggestion that there is one being, Gaia, whose intelligence can guide the world. There is certainly no need to think that humankind has been devised as Gaia's way of coping with some cosmic situation (say, the continuing rise in solar temperature) that less conscious processes cannot manage any more. The speed with which such fantasies take hold is itself significant, but it reveals our human conceit much more than reverence, even when it is couched in apparently self-deprecating ways. Lewis Thomas again: 'We are a living part of Earth's life, owned and operated by the Earth, probably specialized for functions on its behalf that we have not yet glimpsed.'[22] On which more hereafter.

The sense of Gaia as a single, guiding principle is not a scientific one, nor an hypothesis. But maybe it is true: there may, after all, be other modes of knowledge than the scientific. The lesson that the scientific establishment learnt from Enlightenment thinkers – though it is worth saying that none of the latter really taught that lesson – was that reliable, scientific knowledge only came to those who purged themselves of their humanity. We must stop seeing omens and associations everywhere, stop treating phenomena as episodes in some familiar fable, stop reading an intention into everything. Either there were no final causes in the world of nature, or they were not at any rate the ones that ordinarily sensual human beings supposed. 'In seeking to show that Nature does nothing in vain – that is, nothing that is not to man's advantage – they seem to have shown only this, that Nature and the gods are as crazy as mankind.'[23] We must not 'identify' with what goes on, must not be anthropomorphic, participatory, moralistic. Even if there is a kind of beauty in nature (and it would be difficult to exclude such beauty from ordinary scientific theory) it is no human beauty. Things do not serve our ends, or any ends with which we can easily sympathize.

## C Participatory knowledge and the feminine

Ecomystics of the kind I am discussing now seem ready to reverse the progress of the 'Real Philosophy' (which is to say of non-participatory, experimental science). Anti-realists may do so easily, but they are not my present concern. Anti-realist and mystic both alike may point out the hidden metaphors and dubious emotions that lie behind, for example, Bacon's advice to put nature to the question, to haul secrets from the womb of nature, to use her as a wife to make our children and not as a courtesan for pleasure.[24] Even the language of Galileo (who was a greater scientist and philosopher by far) is rich in images of rape and dominion. Twisting Nature from its natural courses, the Baconian scientist is proudly convinced that Nature had no meaning anyway, nor offered any limit to his endeavour. The effort to deny an easy emotional identification is one that leads to a divided soul: the vivisector speaks of 'animal preparations' or 'matter in that state known as living' and acts out the contempt and hatred we all feel for those whom we have injured unforgivably. Refusing emotional identification we must make sure that the creatures we won't identify with know their place.

So non-participatory science has tangled roots: it grows partly from that necessary intellectual discipline of distinguishing what we feel from what others feel. We heterosexual males should not suppose that women are erotically receptive just because our wishes paint them so. But it also grows from mingled disappointment and contempt: if women don't want what we want we can deny that they want anything, and so make them available to us. Instead of denying our emotions, therefore, we should seek to listen to them carefully. The emotionally ill-educated get things wrong, about their human friends, and other animals, and nature itself. It does not follow that they will get things right by declaring all their friendlier emotions liars and leaving themselves at the mercy of their hidden fears and lusts.

The story I have just given, of course, imagines a greater contrast between science, as commonly understood, and mystical insight than is convincing. Others than ecomystics have pointed out the importance of emotional insight, or a sense of beauty, or an unprovable conviction in great science. To refuse to listen to such usual responses is, so Lorenz remarked, as silly as stopping up one's ears. There is nothing very special about scientific insight, even into purely unintended systems: such insight is the product of a complex evolution. Science depends far more on virtues of tolerance, honesty and good sense (all we mean by 'reasonable') than on any particular method of scientific demonstration. We can reason our way to understand the world and its denizens, if indeed we can, because the ways of the world and its denizens are embedded in our very being. We understand by thinking ourselves beneath the skin of friend or domestic dog or sometime prey or the great world itself. Even the most overtly 'materialist' of scientists may admit to thinking themselves inside a photon, or a living cell. Such insights should be checked, but not dismissed as nonsense. Without them we will never understand a thing.

Companionable or convivial understanding is sometimes associated with 'feminine' modes of cognition. 'Masculine' understanding, it is said, is simultaneously abstract and objectifying. Men (biologically or culturally) are trained to ignore their own immediate emotional responses to a situation, to think of it in the way that any disinterested observer might manage, as an example of some very general, abstract principle. What matters to a 'masculine' intelligence is high-principled consistency, and (equivalently) an object purged of any merely subjective, accidental, historical qualities. Knowledge is understood as abstract or expert knowledge, best expressed as a system of interlocking propositions, such that one who knows can 'justify' his knowledge by detailing exactly why things must be as they are believed to be. One anecdote makes the point: in the 1984 Grange Inquiry into a number of infant deaths at a hospital in Toronto, 'when lawyers, who were mostly men, questioned doctors, the questions were phrased in terms of what they *knew*. When nurses were on the stand, the question was "Based on your *experience* ..." Experience in our society is considered second-class compared to knowledge. Nurses should not know.'[25] We ought not to believe anything without the right kind of justification, and all trains of justification should, ideally, begin from self-evident principles which are either logical axioms or reports of immediate, unprejudiced sensory experience. The twin projects of empiricism and rationalism (taking sensory reports or logical axioms as foundational) are in some disarray, not least because the epistemological axiom just stated is pragmatically self-refuting (it being neither logical axiom nor sensory report nor deducible from anything else that is), but 'masculinist' epistemology is still the preferred option amongst educators. The great alternative, the 'feminine' mode, is to reject foundationalist, abstract, systematic epistemology, in favour of more personal modes. Experience, craft-knowledge, educated sensibility are all, in fact, crucial even in self-consciously scientific disciplines. Our knowledge of each other's life and meaning is always of this kind. We cannot *know* without putting ourselves 'at risk' (or what seems risk) in a personal encounter. We cannot know without accepting our dependent status, as inheritors of a tradition and as faced by truths we should acknowledge.

'Feminine' or 'tacit' knowledge may be especially relevant in environmentalism, for two reasons. The first has to do with the issues already addressed: whereas the abstract, objectifying form of knowledge tends to identify its object as outside value, or even (speciously) without value, more personalized modes of knowing cannot make this error. We know someone or something best when we can comfortably live with them. This mode of knowing does not aspire to leaving things as they are, as if we could *know* only what is not affected by our knowing. Knowing is an ongoing project, a dance of mutual accommodation, not a pretended separation of subject and object which is magically transcended through the subject's power. That model of knowledge is grotesque. It is absurd, as I have said before, to postulate a world of 'pure matter', having no necessary qualities or values and then express surprise that qualities and values cannot be explained in terms referring only to that 'pure matter'. It is just as absurd to postulate a subject divorced from any object and then pretend that the subject could still have an accurate picture of the object. Matter that does not have any mental aspect cannot explain mind; subjects that are not united with their objects cannot know that what they have is knowledge. Real knowledge must arise from union, as minds arise from a world that never was 'pure matter'. It follows that the model of the earth and its inhabitants that is abstracted from our personal response to the organic world is an idol. 'The Great Mother has been won back to life.'

The second feature of this methodology is a distrust of the demand for proof. What cannot be 'proved', by more abstract canons, should not be believed: from which it follows, in practice, that what cannot be proved is disbelieved, even though its contradictory is also unprovable. If we cannot 'prove' that unanaesthetized dogs 'feel pain' we are entitled to assume that they do not even though this is just as far from proven. Clearly we cannot prove that they feel pain if 'proof' requires us to deduce that they must feel pain from logical axioms, mathematical theorems, physical laws and sensory reports, all of which have been carefully phrased to avoid any reference to the 'unknown' inner life of dogs or anything else. But 'proof' is suspect for another reason. It may sometimes be right to demand certain kinds of 'proof'. What is admissible in a court of law often does depend on our experience of errors: eye-witnesses, and expert witnesses, have been mistaken, especially when they have let their moral fury or prejudice dictate what they report. But some rules of evidence may – all too obviously – favour one side or other. If rape cannot be 'proved' without an independent witness few rapists will be convicted. If the cause of infant leukaemia near a nuclear installation, or of one particular incident, cannot be 'proved' to be the radiation around the site, unless all other explanations are ruled out, then no one will win compensation for what – commonsensically – must be an injury. To 'prove' is to compel particular people to act upon a certain theory, and the engines of proof, of such compulsion, are in the hands of (largely male) authority. For example, as long as the Soviet authorities held all the cards it was impossible to 'prove' what damage they were doing: nothing at all could count as 'proof' that they were lying scoundrels. Even the most ardent radical can agree (and should) that the West is not so wicked, nor so damaging, as that 75-year experiment. But even if that regime was worse than anything the West has done it is difficult not to suspect that there can be no true proofs until political and economic power is more equal. 'Proving', till then, is always an exercise of power, and the harder it is made to 'prove' a thesis the less such changes will occur. The case of Freud is one that I cited earlier.

Environmentalists of this kind put more trust in the reports of those immediately involved with the living world than in the predictions of abstract theoreticians. The testimony and fears of indigenous peoples, the empathetic understanding of (some) women, artists and craftspeople, the suspicions of those who are likeliest to suffer the effects of novel engineering projects – all are given more weight than they would be by more conventional standards. It is not enough to reply to environmentalist fears by saying that our present meteorological and evolutionary models are as yet too crude to prove any particular prediction (and we are therefore entitled to believe, without proof, what suits the prosperous to have us all believe). It is not enough to explain those fears away by suggesting that they are projections of personal or social inadequacies (of which the spokesmen for the prosperous are free). It is certainly not enough to say that our present health and prosperity, greater by far than that of any generation until now, must 'prove' that we are doing something right (and should go on). We should be at least as suspicious of those who defend the uses of power as we are of those who attack them. We should be at least as suspicious of those who demand 'proof' while making it impossible to provide such proof, as we are of those who demand that the sentence should precede the trial. What counts in knowledge, as it counts in any responsible politics, is to build towards a genuinely convivial culture, which does not outlaw anyone's experience of life. There is a role for system, and for objectivity: neither can long survive, or be worth having, outside the personal, unsystematized and value-laden Knowing that is – not our foundation, but – our home.

Those who have lived longest together, in attempted love and honesty, should be given credit for knowing each other well. Those who have lived and worked with animals have far better evidence for what they say than any armchair theoreticians who pretend that animals could, in the abstract, go through identical motions without meaning anything. The strange resurgence amongst armchair philosophers of Descartes' least plausible thesis (that non-human animals are insensible) is usually linked with a crass verificationism that is otherwise outmoded, an unargued claim about the impossibility of non-verbal thought that makes the acquisition of language a constant miracle, and of course a deep unwillingness to admit that we mistreat our cousins (which was also Descartes' plea). Those who live close to the earth should be respected when they claim to feel the earth's inwardness, even if the abstract, scientific theory does not wholly prove them right. So far, so ecomystical. The problem is, one problem is, to recognize who *does* live 'close to the earth'. That this form of knowing should be reckoned feminine is not wholly absurd, but the feminists that I have read do not strike me as certain candidates for Gaian sainthood. That does not mean that they are not such saints.

So what have ecofeminists to contribute here? What is the connection between the status and state of women and the status and state of Gaia? Why, correspondingly, does it seem appropriate to speak of 'Gaia' or 'Mother Earth' at all? Why is Nature imaged as a woman? Why are women felt, by some, to be especially close to nature? An earlier generation of feminists would have disdained the association: what is it but a pretext to exclude women from the sphere of science, law and culture, even indeed from properly moral responsibility? You can't call women 'weak-willed', Aristotle said, because no one could expect them to control their passions. Mother-love is instinctive and unreasoning. Women are incapable of abstract reasoning. I confess that I regard this sort of thing as pernicious drivel – which is the kind of remark that, quoted out of context, earned me the reputation of unreasonable polemicist! But a newer generation of feminists have decided to accept these charges, and to redescribe them. If women, biologically or culturally, have been excluded from the disciplines of abstract reasoning and encouraged instead to rely upon womanly intuition, gut-feeling, concrete appreciation of particular cases, that is to their advantage. Carol Gilligan's investigation of modes of moral reasoning is to the point.[26] If abstract moral problems are posed men most often employ and urgently defend particular abstract principles (as 'it's wrong to steal even for good ends' or 'human life is more important than mere property'). Women most often insist on treating the abstract problem as a concrete case, and seek to discover solutions that evade the moral crux. Women, one could say, are much more used to conciliation, men to opposition; women must make do, and men stand on their principles; women's care is given to concrete individuals, men's to flags and systems. Primavesi instances the Indian 'Hug-the-trees' movement as an example of such empowerment by loving attention to individual trees.[27]

The contrast is not an exact one, though it is supported by my experience of teaching moral philosophy. To call it exact or absolute, of course, would be a surrender to more 'masculinist' modes of thought: the truth is always more interesting. Concrete and conciliatory reasoning is not impossible for men; abstract and acute dichotomies are not impossible for women. To suppose otherwise, and fall into the habit of praising women for being illogical, however important it may be to distinguish right reason from merely abstract and intolerant logicism, is dangerous. Jacquetta Hawkes' fable *The Woman As Great As the World*[28] depicts a fabulous woman, lounging unconcernedly among the clouds, occasionally impregnated by 'the Wind', and giving birth to all the creatures of the world. The final birth is of people, who bring her the same self-consciousness that she had briefly experienced in the Wind's embrace, encourage her to try to argue logically with the Wind, and so quarrel with him, and at last annoy her so much that she destroys them all in gales of laughter. The unconcealed inhumanism of this image will concern me later: what matters here is the profound hostility to women, ordinary women, it reveals. 'Real women' should be earthy, inconsiderate and self-absorbed, never troubling their pretty heads about the results of what they do, or their reasons for so doing. And if that is what they are then Aristotle was quite right to think they needed male protectors. As Ursula King remarks, it is partly because Indian thought judges that women have the greater power that they are, in practice, subordinated to men. Much the same can be said of ancient Greek society, and maybe others.[29] I can only repeat that this is pernicious drivel.

Nonetheless, there is something to be said for a relatively 'feminine' mode of ecological reasoning. The chief moral of ecology, even in its least mystical, most atomistic form, is that we must reckon with multiple causality. We live within a network, not on a single line. What matters is keeping the show on the road, not arguing about abstract rights or an equally abstract utility. Large-scale or unprecedented actions are unwise; relying unsuspiciously on expert opinion is unwise; treating any elements of the one undivided biosphere as enemies is unwise. Right action is delicate, traditional, conciliatory and unassuming. Doris Lessing's comic masterpiece *The Sentimental Agents in the Volyen Empire* assigns one of the few sensible actions of the book not to the well-intentioned, self-important leader, but to an ordinary woman – ordinary not in that pernicious sense so readily evoked by Hawkes, but in her attention to the actual needs of those she cares for, and the possibility of small and yet significant improvements.

And to place that sensible advice in a religious context once again: those who would do good, must do it in minute particulars. The sacred that we must wake up to serve will show itself at hand, and not in distant dreams. Correspondingly, we should not let ourselves be sandbagged by the rhetoric of 'crisis': there are innumerable little crises, even if they often depend on one thing. There are also innumerable little solutions. That is one real force of the idea of immanence or incarnation, though I shall be insisting at a later point that there is equal strength and importance in the idea of transcendence. Similarly, if 'Gaia' is a proper icon of divinity, we must remember that she does not stand apart from us, because we cannot stand apart from her. The 'environment' is not something that straightforwardly environs us: the term is a misleading, and revealing one for what surrounds and sustains us too. Even if the notion of our functional significance is romantic, and complacent, it is still true that we are indeed 'the rocks dancing'. I do believe that there is a place for quietness, for a willingness to 'listen' to what the great world is saying in and around us, for preferring delicate adjustments to large-scale alterations. In all this men can learn from women – but also the civilized and affluent can learn from 'primitives' and the poor.


## D  The practical effect

Remarks like that are truisms, and may of course conceal all manner of self-deceptions. We have a long tradition of admiring poverty and what we think 'primitive' – but only from a distance. And this hypocrisy can easily find arguments. For the problem is that it is not easy to move from vaguely pantheistic, participatory theories of the earth even to the actions that people adopt pantheism to promote. It is important to see the earth and her denizens as sacred if we are to avoid catastrophe. It is important to realize that we are not distinct from the earth, but truly part of her, and 'when we spit upon the ground we spit upon ourselves', as Chief Seattle probably did not say. But if we are part of the earth, why aren't our lives and practices as sacred as any other? Jeffers' inhumanist:[30]

> 'It is ignoble', he said, 'and nearly senseless to pray for anything,
> But in so great and righteous a cause – hear me,
> Lord God! Exterminate
> The race of man. For man only in the world, except a few kinds of insect, is
> essentially cruel.
> Therefore slay also these if you will: the driver ant,
> And the slave-maker ant, and the slick wasp
> That paralyzes living meat for her brood: but first

The human race. Cut it off, sear the stump.' So he prayed, being old and childish,
  and the Lord answered him
Out of the driving storm: 'I will, but not now.'

The choice seems absolute. Either we think that Nature, or especially the living earth, is perfect as she is, or we do not. If we do, and somehow adjust ourselves to the amoral rapture with which television documentaries now greet the spectacle of wasp grubs eating living caterpillars or wild dogs tearing at a living antelope, then why should we make exceptions for the greatest living predator? Nature maintains herself in the exchange of materials, constantly adjusting to the change of days. She, so to speak, raises no objections to slave-maker ants, ichneumon wasps or chimpanzees who batter in the skulls of young baboons – or chimpanzees. So why should we, who revere her, raise objections to human predation and control? Is the claim that we can see disastrous results from our unfettered action? But doesn't that imply that Nature can make mistakes, that rational folk like us are duty bound to correct her? And how then can her ways be sacred? Must we not really entertain the thought that things would be better if we (or somebody) controlled the world?

Again: it certainly feels significant when Leopold, for example, says that 'a thing is right when it tends to preserve the integrity, stability and beauty of the biotic community . . . (and) wrong when it tends otherwise'.[31] But it is not clear how any particular state of the whole is better, more integrated, more stable or more beautiful than any other. According to Lovelock's estimate[32] Gaia was more densely inhabited, and better balanced, during the ice ages. But even that thought, humbling though it may be, can be challenged. If Gaia has survived this long it will even survive us, and be no worse for any biochemical changes it thereby endures. There is scope for 'thinking like a mountain', but when is a mountain better or worse off? When we think like a mountain, must we regret erosion, deforestation or mining work? That Nature, Gaia, is a goddess is actually what lies behind some of our silliest practices: because we think her divine, we think her indefatigably purifying, and pump wastes and novel poisons into the earth and water in expectation of a good return.

The unfortunate conclusion of Nature-worship, despite the many insights of its devotees, is bloodier and less responsive than the domineering creeds of former humanists. It is at least worth noticing that ecofeminists, who begin by deprecating patriarchal images of God as the Lord of Battles, seem to conclude by praising Kali or Anat.[33] At least the God of the Hebrews does not rejoice in the blood of His enemies or children. Those who worship Nature are not far away from Moloch.

## Notes

1. See Iris Murdoch, *The Sovereignty of Good* (Routledge & Kegan Paul: London, 1970); *The Levinas Reader* (Blackwell: Oxford, 1989), S. Hand (ed.).

2. See John B. Cobb, *Process Theology as Political Theology* (Manchester University Press: Manchester, 1982), p. 6.

3. Starhawk, *Dreaming the Dark* (Unwin Hyman: London, 1990), p. 11.

4. The word is R. M. Hare's.

5. 'A value which is only posited by man has no right to demand that I should sacrifice my existence to it': K. Heim, *Christian Faith and Natural Science*, tr. N. H. Smith (SCM Press: London, 1953), p. 184.

6. See C. Merchant, *The Death of Nature*, (Wildwood House: London, 1982) p. 41.

7. Quoted by Starhawk, *Dreaming the Dark*, p. 24.

8. Ian Bradley, *God Is Green* (Darton, Longman & Todd: London, 1990), p. 14: is there *any* evidence for this?

9. See Judith L. Boire, *At One with All Life* (Findhorn Press: Forres, 1990).

10. R. Hutton, *Pagan Religions of the Ancient British Isles* (Blackwell: Oxford, 1991), pp. 306, 370 note 37.

11. Hutton, ibid., p. 304.

12. Hutton, ibid., pp. 37f.

13. Matthew Fox, *Creation Spirituality* (Harper: San Francisco, 1991), p. 7.

14. Notably, Olbers' Paradox, and Bentley's: an infinite and homogenous universe (however sparsely inhabited) would exert an infinite gravitational force, and be infinitely bright, at every point.

15. Lewis Thomas, *The Lives of a Cell* (Penguin: Harmondsworth, 1978; 1st edn 1974), p. 53.

16. F. P. Ramsey, *Foundations of Mathematics* (Routledge and Kegan Paul: London, 1931), pp. 35f.; see my *From Athens to Jerusalem* (Clarendon Press: Oxford, 1984), p. 122.

17. Thomas, *Lives of a Cell*, pp. 145f.

18. See J. Lovelock, *The Ages of Gaia* (Oxford University Press: Oxford, 1988).

19. R. Dawkins, *The Selfish Gene* (Oxford University Press: Oxford, 1976);

E. O. Wilson, *Sociobiology: a New Synthesis* (Harvard University Press Cambridge, MA: 1975).

20. S. J. Gould; cited in Peter Bunyard and Edward Goldsmith (eds), *Gaia: The Thesis, the Mechanism and the Implications* (Wadebridge Ecological Centre, 1989).

21. Such uses have been discussed by Andrew Brennan, *Thinking About Nature* (Routledge: London, 1988); see also R. Elliott (ed.), *Environmental Ethics* (Clarendon Press: Oxford, forthcoming).

22. L. Thomas, cited by Charlene Spretnak and F. Capra, *Green Politics* (Paladin: London, 1985), p. 234.

23. B. Spinoza, *Ethics* I, appendix: tr. S. Shirley, ed. S. Feldman (Hackett Publishing Co: Indianapolis, 1982), p. 58.

24. See Merchant, *Death of Nature*, pp. 164ff.

25. Alice Baumgart in *Canadian Nurse* (1985), cited by L. Code, 'Credibility: a double standard' in L. Code, S. Mullett and C. Overall (eds), *Feminist Perspectives: Philosophical Essays on Method and Morals* (Toronto: University of Toronto Press, 1988), pp. 64–88: 64.

26. C. Gilligan, *In a Different Voice: Psychological Theory and Women's Development* (Harvard University Press: Cambridge MA, 1982).

27. A. Primavesi, *From Apocalypse to Genesis* (Burns & Oates: Tunbridge Wells, 1991), p. 60.

28. J. Hawkes, *The Woman As Great As the World* (Random House: New York 1953); anthologized in P. Shepard and D. McKinley (eds), *The Subversive Science* (Houghton Mifflin: Boston, 1969).

29. U. King: cited by Primavesi, *Apocalypse to Genesis*, p. 61.

30. R. Jeffers, *The Double Axe and Other Poems* (Liveright: New York, 1977), p. 110.

31. A. Leopold, *A Sand County Almanac* (OUP: New York, 1949), pp. 224f.

32. J. Lovelock, *The Ages of Gaia* (OUP; Oxford, 1988), pp. 136ff.

33. See S. Heine, *Christianity and the Goddesses*, tr. J. Bowker (SCM: London, 1988), p. 46.

# Blood and soil

. . . . . . . . . . . . . . . . . . . . . . . . . . . . . .

### A How to pollute the landscape

It is clear enough that moralizing sentimentalism serves human ends.
We demean the real dignity of other creatures by dressing them up in
fact or fantasy as furry people. That is the real strength of methodo-
logical objectivism: it spares us easy misconstruals of what others do.
The kind of inhumanism to which I have referred follows a subtly
different route. Instead of reading final goals and moral commonplace into natural events, the inhumanist draws her goals and moral-
isms from a nature viewed as utterly indifferent to ordinary human
ways. If nature is non-anthropocentric we should be so too. Jeffers
again:

> Whatever we do to a landscape – even to look – damages it.
> Even Niagara becomes ridiculous![1]

Our aim should be to glimpse the world as it would be, as it is,
without our gaze, to cool ourselves on the bare fact.[2]

One of the many oddities of modern rhetoric is that 'dualism',
in any form, is reckoned damnable – except when it appears as
inhumanism or devout indifferentism. By any ordinary account
inhumanism is plainly dualistic: on the one hand, the bare truth
intuited by those who dare to step beyond the bourgeois comforts of

their ordinary selves, and on the other, the world as human landscape and environment. In place of anti-realist insistence that the human landscape must be all the world, inhumanists propose that we, even if not yet God, destroy the human.

> People are a mistake. The Universe would be sweeter and fresher without them. When the morning dew sparkles like diamonds . . . there is beauty and exquisite purity in each blade of grass and it is dreadful to think of the beauty beheld by sinful eyes, which smirch its loveliness with their sordid and cruel ambitions. I cannot understand how God . . . can have tolerated so long the baseness of those who boast blasphemously that they have been made in his image.[3]

The words are Russell's, who is better known, perhaps, for his somewhat pretentious defiance of Omnipotent Matter in the name of those same sinful, self-regarding eyes. But I should not give the impression that only consciously non-Christian authors had the thought. Simone Weil speaks of the beauty of a landscape just when no one looks at it. 'When I am anywhere, I pollute the silence of earth and sky with my breathing and the beating of my heart.'[4] There is a real strength in this vision. Because of what we are we cannot allow things their being: everything becomes 'environment', tools, things-for-us. In denying one kind of dualism the inhumanist accepts another: the little human animals are as much a part of undivided and inhuman fact as any other. In seeking to intuit the landscape as it is when no one looks at it, no one puts boundary markers or plans or memories upon it, we must seek to intuit our very selves as they are when no one looks at them. We must somehow achieve a glimmer of that un-selfconsciousness that is the secret, so we are told, of natural purity and grace. That vision must be utterly distinct from our ordinary consciousness and yet be of the very things that are thus ordinarily conscious. To know without remembering that we know: that is the impossible condition of being in harmony with nature. The task is impossible except by sudden grace: we cannot set ourselves the task of letting Being be and hope to recognize our own success in this. Those who know don't speak – except as part of their unselfconscious practice.

The unselfconscious sage, if such there are, will do just what comes naturally, because what the sage does has not been restricted or perverted by self-conscious thought or judgement. The sage may treat the people as straw dogs. If enlightenment consists in not-getting-in-the-way of nature, then there seems good reason for us unenlightened folk to fear the sage. What happens naturally includes disaster and predation. It is childish, as Jeffers said, to complain about how insects behave, or mammals. That he himself complained most bitterly – for example about a vain paralytic's taking the States into a European war (the words are his) – makes sense only as a poetic gesture. Perhaps the people, being duped, had a false idea about what they were doing. Perhaps instead of choosing to avenge or right a wrong the battling armies were like warrior ants, and erred only in their belief. Yet having such beliefs, having high purposes and self-praising judgements, is just what people do: 'We are what we are, and might remember not to hate any person . . . and not to fear death; it is the only way to be cleansed.'[5]

This deeply ecomystical ideal, by diminishing our human self-conceit, may halt some invasive practices. It may also encourage an uncritical reliance on invasive practice. Maybe inhumanists will not harry the world to make themselves feel great, nor seek to 'better' humankind because they think such benefits 'deserved'. But maybe they will harry the world like any other predator, licensed like wolves or magpies or killer whales to make our use of what's available. The net effect must very likely be that inhumanists will praise and imitate the predator. Jeffers, so far as can be seen, did not, and the collapse of his popularity when he was seen to have attacked the Allies' effort or defended Hitler as a 'tragic figure' was, perhaps, an example of that war-fever he decried. I remain doubtful that he had any grounds for despising militarists, and troubled by his occasional assaults, verbal as they were, on ordinarily sinful people.

Jeffers and many other writers of the 1930s gave expression to a real religious possibility, of killing off the sensual self in favour of a willed reversion to unselfconscious nature: 'unselfconscious' precisely in that we would then be conscious of a greater self and being for which our previous thoughts and fancies would seem at once absurd and necessary. Zaehner traced the vision from Parmenides to Manson,[6] and might have identified many more intellectuals as its devotees. Olaf Stapledon was Merseyside's contribution. The obvious association, however, and one of the most troubling for environmentalists, is National Socialism.

## B National Socialism and the religion of nature

Spretnak and Capra, commenting on German Greens, report that 'when the Greens speak with reverence of a subtle connection to the

Earth and nature, older Germans are reminded of the Nazi teaching that the German soil is sacred, as is her "superrace" of citizens'.[7] I fear that the association is more than an historical accident, and that other familiar elements of Nazism are also relevant to any serious examination of environmentalism. I certainly don't mean that 'deep ecology' is therefore irrecoverably tainted.

> National Socialist ideologues were in no small way concerned that man, or at least some men, live in harmony with the environment and, appreciating the fact that this is obviously necessary, we must recognize that just because something happens to have been emphasised by people as despicable as the Nazis does not make it wrong.[8]

But we need to see more clearly why 'living in harmony' is necessary, and what it means.

Deep ecologism and Nazis are alike in their rejection of ordinary objectivism. 'There is no inorganic nature, there is no dead, mechanical earth. The Great Mother has been won back to life.'[9] Scientistic objectivism postulates a value-neutral and finally incomprehensible universe, over against which stands the human intellect and will. Denying that division between a real world and a human one, some thinkers ended as anti-realists (as I have shown before) and others as inhumanists. They sought to identify with, to be absorbed in the one world, conceived as an organic living whole. The ideal must be: not to stand apart from the living earth, even in fantasy. Self-consciousness and objectivity, considered as a disciplined attempt to stand aside from what 'comes naturally', are anathematized. The proper mode of thought, if only we can recover it, is that of peasants deeply rooted in the soil (and therefore unable even to recognize that so they are). So we turn full circle. On the one hand, the one world will one day be engulfed by fire or ice, and has no time to spare for bourgeois notions of benevolence or mercy or human dignity. There is no other world than this, and realism requires us to identify with that one world, dispensing with anthropocentric and self-serving fantasies. On the other hand, in rejecting self-consciousness we must admire those people who have never thought of a world apart from the world they live. The intellectual élite seek to fill their minds entirely with a vision of the one inhuman world; the peasantry uncritically inhabit a world imbued with what objectivists had reckoned to be projections. Along with the Great Mother, 'who does nothing and does not care, [who] alone is seriously there',[10] there emerge the gods of local spring and spinney, blood, fire and harvest. The old German proverb said that 'city air makes free': in place of freedom Darré, Hitler's sometime Minister of Agriculture, proposed Blood and Soil, a peasantry united with the land, in harmony with nature. Neither peasants nor the intellectual élite could conceive of moral absolutes or ideals not fully embodied in the natural world.

The ideologues of National Socialism were certainly confused and often incoherent: that, after all, is what one must expect when the laws of logic, let alone humanity, are denounced as 'anti-life'. That Heidegger – notoriously – avowed his support for the Nazis as of the essence of his own philosophy, and later confessed only that he had mistaken a symptom of 'modern man's disease' for its awaited cure, should not be forgotten, but can, perhaps, be understood. Heidegger hoped to heal a breach, between human experience and the objective world, but lent his support to a programme that crudely and appallingly concluded the tendency he had identified: to treat human beings as matter in Cartesian motion, or else – equivalently – as compost.

This almost unintelligible picture of reality – unintelligible because devotedly unintelligent – may help to explain why anti-Semitism was not an historical accident. Hitler was, in his terms, right to suspect the Jews as enemies of his vision, and for several reasons. Jews could not be embedded in the land and still be living Jews: here they, literally, had no continuing city and their devotion must be to a Place elsewhere. Like many other of the Nazi themes, this was a common enough one, and one of the roots of Zionism: perhaps Jews would not be hated if they 'returned' to a literal land and became like other nations. But they were not just wanderers, as Gypsies were. They were believed to exercise control of an international, capitalistic kind: such capitalism transformed proper 'organic' relationships of give and take into abstract, mechanical transactions. Worse still, their ancestral creed – with which they had infected Christendom – demanded ideal justice, recognized individual dignity and spoke for the land and humankind alike as creatures, servants of the Lord. Hitler seems also to have believed the common libel that Jewish thought and practice were indifferent to animals. 'How can you find any pleasure', he asked Felix Kersten, 'in shooting behind cover at poor creatures browsing on the edge of a wood, innocent, defenceless and unsuspecting? Properly considered it's pure murder. . . . Nature is so marvellously beautiful and every animal has a right to live. . . . You will find this respect for animals in all Indo-Germanic peoples.'[11]

Was that just self-deception or hypocrisy? If every animal has a right to live, do not Jewish animals? The doctors who participated in the mass murder of Jews, Gypsies, homosexuals, the incurably sick or mentally retarded were applying to human animals the lessons they had learnt in animal laboratories across the West: to disregard merely sentimental reactions to the plight of living organisms from which they distinguished themselves. It was a lesson that others, even non-Germans, had already applied. One of Chesterton's common themes is the misuse of medical judgement to incarcerate – and experiment upon – eccentrics: no one who has attended to what has happened in this century can think this concern absurd. Canavan has identified one episode in particular, involving Cyril Burt (whom Chesterton criticized): in an article of 1950 Burt recalled how 'with the advent of compulsory education' there was medical concern about 'mental deficiency', which was perhaps attributable to small skull size. Burt remarks without comment or apology that of those children of the poor subjected to craniectomy 25 per cent died and the rest showed no mental improvement.[12] The reader, Canavan goes on to say,

> can perhaps understand Chesterton's anger at a system of social reform that delivered the defenceless poor of the country into the hands of doctors who could try out their theories on these human guinea pigs and take children from their parents on grounds of arbitrarily assessed 'mental deficiency' – in order to subject them to appalling and futile operations as a result of which twenty-five per cent died and even those who survived showed no improvement.

Consider also the eugenicist claptrap which spoke of 'denying the right of scum to beget millions of their kind'.[13] This is why Chesterton speaks so harshly of 'philanthropy', not because he was a romantic egoist but because he knew rather better than his present-day critics what that involved.

> Because you could not even yawn
> When your Committees would prepare
> To have the teeth of paupers drawn,
> Or strip the slums of Human Hair;
> Because a Doctor Otto Maehr
> Spoke of a 'segregated few' –
> And you sat smiling in your chair –
> It shall not be forgiven you.[14]

Nazism, in brief, was not an anomaly, an atavism, but a deliberate acting-out, to the bitter end, of proposals emanating from some of the most respected of European intellectuals. And although confusion and double-think were rife amongst the intellectuals, I fear that they had an answer to the charge of obvious inconsistency with respect to animals and Jews. For the élite Jews and the rest weren't animals: they were not whole creatures living in the world. Nazis projected onto them the very image of bacterial infection that so often surfaces in ecomystical debate. Jews weren't real creatures, but cunning automata, lacking human and animal souls: this was 'proved' by the detachment, isolation and abject submission that the Nazis managed to induce in some of their victims.

> The National Socialists had succeeded in creating that which they knew existed all along. Through degradation, humiliation, torture and total dehumanization they had created the non-human, in fact non-natural Jewish enemy, seemingly incapable of feeling those normal, human emotions that were characteristic of those decent folk engaged in annihilating them.[15]

Callicott, an environmentalist with rather little sympathy for animal liberation, similarly adduces the degraded state of factory-farmed animals to 'prove' that they are not real creatures worthy of respect.[16]

The Nazis projected the image of bacterial infection on the Jews, and strove to conform them to that image. What is alarming about all this for any would-be environmentalist is that modern rhetoric conjoins exactly those ideas. On the one hand, despite a thousand scholarly and theological rebuttals, we are constantly told that the ecological crisis is the consequence of Jewish thought. On the other, the image of humankind as a sort of bacterial infection or a plague of vermin constantly reappears. We avoid being vermin ourselves, even in fantasy, by separating ourselves from those in whom the verminous character is believed intrinsic. Gloating descriptions of plague, famine, war by which inhuman Nature will control her brood, leave the rock pure, demolish fantasies of universal justice: these project upon the future, upon Jews, or homosexuals, the very fate that eco-mystics of this kind must otherwise fear for themselves. When the EarthFirst! group suggest that epidemics such as AIDS are a way of solving the population problem they lend weight to the suspicion that 'ecologism' is genocidal.[17] When this sort of thing is yoked with a profound distrust of international business and the money-market, symbolically identified with Jews, it is hardly surprising that older Europeans look askance at ecomystical propaganda. Whatever solution it is we need to our present and continuing crisis, let it not, please God, be that. *Pace* Toynbee, the religion we do not need to embrace is 'pantheism, as exemplified in Shinto' – or, as Daisatsu

Ikeda at once pointed out to him, in even less agreeable creeds.[18] 'It is just this underhanded assault on the universal culture which all humanists who sincerely believe in the unity of mankind and in the possibility of a free and just society must strongly deplore.'[19]

## C Global or bioregional authorities?

But I must still believe, with Blake, that every thing possible to be believed is an image of the truth.[20] No such images should be worshipped in preference to truth, but any may, if we approach it properly, be epiphanic. What truth is it that hides in inhumanism and national feeling? Is it after all, when properly understood, a resource we would do wrong to throw away?

What reason do we have to preserve the land and its inhabitants? The question is, of course and quite deliberately, absurd. 'The nation that destroys its soil destroys itself':[21] a remark of Franklin Roosevelt's that might equally have been Darré's. Darré indeed found inspiration in Roosevelt's measures against land erosion. Whatever fantasies some may entertain of constructing new habitats among the asteroids, or at Earth's Trojan points, we have no other life-support system than this earth. In the past great empires could survive by destroying other people's soil instead. In the past small agricultural bands could practise slash-and-burn and still be confident that the soil would have repaired itself behind them by the time they came around again. None of this is true for us. Of course improved techniques can push the limits back: we can keep land fertile by careful use of the earth's capital, composted forests turned into petroleum. But though we constantly postpone the payment, it will come. What is difficult, as I declared in my first chapter, is to keep this fact alive and somehow avoid the tragedy of the commons. We need, remember, a religion, a morale. Even a world state, a Global Ecological Authority with absolute power to resettle populations, restrict the use of energy and defend the habitats on whose survival all our futures rest, could not govern only by the sword. The military means, after all, are very expensive in energy and labour: the more difficult the decisions GEA takes, the more resentment subject populations feel, the more resources GEA must divert to military ends. Almost the only way to harness people in the military mode is to construct a war between opposing powers that will each seem abominable to the other's peoples but will actually do exactly the same things (as

Orwell saw). Nor is there reason to believe that GEA's decisions would be sound ones: without a genuine religion, something to bind their hearts to causes and commitments larger than their little lives, GEA's officials would undoubtedly begin to act, or refrain from acting, just to save themselves. Even if they had some wider cause, of course, their global decisions would probably be wrong (since none of us can have such accurate information or powers of prophecy as would be needed to avoid appalling errors). The state of Eastern Europe, gradually revealed, should put an end to all collectivist pretensions. Granted that 'the earth is given as a common stock for man to labor & live on',[22] yet that common stock is better managed piecemeal. 'It is by dividing and subdividing these republics from the great National one down thr' all its subordinations, until it ends in the administration of every man's farm and affairs by himself; by placing under every one what his own eye may superintend, that all will be done for the best.'[23]

What a strange idea.

> There is apparently something elvish and fantastic about saying that when capital has come to be too much in the hands of the few, the right thing is to restore it into the hands of the many. The socialist would put it into the hands of even fewer; but those people would be politicians, who (as we know) always administer it in the interests of the many.[24]

I shall address the seemingly individualist implication of this distributism at a later point. Here what matters are the little republics that lie between a notional GEA and the single person.

Even to make GEA work we would need a religion, and GEA would probably not work anyway. One option might be a world divided (save at the very top) by war: people would be encouraged in their self-denial by the thought that they must oppose some dreadful enemy, who would actually be the subjects of just such another ruler. Another option might be the Pharaonic: if the rulers could persuade us all that they were gods, and thereby kept control of irrigation, fuels, transport and communication, we might relearn the obedience that maintained Egypt, and the Inca empire, for so long. It would probably embody a caste system, an hereditary bureaucracy, a fierce refusal of all heresies (which is to say, all private choices). But such stability, even if it could be achieved, might not be for the best. Neither a contrived war, nor a new Pharaoh, seems likely, in fact, to persuade us all here-now. If such things happen, it will be after almost-the-worst has happened, and our survivors desperate to make amends. In the meantime the main alternative perhaps is local action, local devotion, 'bioregionalism',[25] or (bluntly) nationalism.

Nationalism has a bad reputation – unless the nations are known to have been oppressed by those of European descent. It might well serve to provide the emotional energy that would be needed for the kind of contrived war I mentioned. It might also serve to keep us quarrelling while the world unravels. But a genuine nationalism need have neither effect. Why should a nation, founded in the love of one particular place and seeking to provide a home for all its kin, persist in seizing land from others who are as deeply attached to it? Nationalism is not necessarily imperial: those who love their country do not necessarily deny the right of other nationals to love their own, nor reckon that their country stands above all others. Of course some do deny that right. The kind of empire that the French have preferred to think they ruled was founded in the assumption that everyone should be French, and forget their past identities. The kind that the English liked to think they ruled was founded in a readiness to allow all other nations an *inferior* place, as long as they conceded that the (southern) English way was best. The kind that enthusiasts for Kant's world-state prefer to think they'd rule is founded in an idea, and not (they say) a prejudice. But it is the very mark of ideologues to think that what they think is obvious: people who think they know what 'reason' rules are generally (or so their victims think) enacting a class or national prejudice that they don't know they have. Some empires openly declare themselves the possession of a dominant class; others pretend to be what any rational person would require, but are actually ruled according to the tenets of one dominant class. It might be best instead to lay down rules preventing the emergence of any such imperial power: to say, in fact, that nations should, as far as decently possible, be independent.

Those who live upon and in a land will be alert to its decay, and are much likelier to care for it than strangers are. Inevitably, what they care for is more than biological. Nature, as such, knows no national boundaries: even island nations are not as separate as their rhetoric imagines. In caring for our land we dare not damage other lands (because what wastes we pour into their air and water will return to us), and may even come, by sympathy, to feel our neighbours' care for their land. In caring for our fragment of the earth we are, exactly, caring for a fragment, something that cannot endure without its neighbours. But it does not follow that the boundaries are unreal, that our care must or should extend at once to all the globe, for most of which we cannot be responsible. The land we care for is a land imbued with memories. 'Primitive' peoples, it is often said, feel for their land in ways that 'Westerners' do not: the Kikuyu were traumatized by their eviction; the Masai carried the names of hills and rivers with them in a desperate attempt to keep themselves together;[26] Chief Seattle probably *did* say that the land, round Pugin Sound, that his people were asked, commanded, to give up was full of their ancestors. 'By the waters of Babylon we sat down and wept when we remembered thee, O Sion . . . How shall we sing the Lord's song in a strange land?'[27] The land that any settled people inhabit is a vast mnemonic: our personal and national memories are bound up in its elements as we experience them. Any alteration or destruction is a little death, and sets ghosts roaming homeless till they are forgotten. 'The land itself is the cathedral at which we are urged to worship.'[28] This is why it is not quite ridiculous to resent the destruction even of quite recent habitats. It may be that the landscape of the Scottish Highlands, or East Anglia, or what you will was actually constructed by past human action (deeply resented, with good reason, at the time).[29] But they now embody local and national memory, as well as being natural habitats for the incoming wild things, and now deserve protection. We may similarly wish to keep the bullet holes from Cromwell's soldiers' desecration of a church.

What is actually now there deserves protection. But aren't there limits? And must there not be limits to what any national group is actually allowed to do?

> Even to the Mere of Dead Faces some haggard phantom of green spring would come; but here neither spring nor summer would ever come again. Here nothing lived, not even the leprous growths that feed on rottenness. The gasping pools were choked with ash and crawling muds, sickly white and grey, as if the mountains had vomited the filth of their entrails upon the lands about. High mounds of crushed and powdered rock, great cones of earth fire-blasted and poison-stained, stood like an obscene graveyard in endless rows, slowly revealed in the reluctant light. They [Frodo and Sam] had come to the desolation that lay before Mordor: the lasting monument to the dark labour of its slaves that should endure when all their purposes were made void; a land defiled, diseased beyond all healing – unless the Great Sea should enter it and wash it with oblivion.[30]

Here is an altered landscape, embodying real memory and doubtless, to a suitably enchanted eye, some beauty of contrasting colours which yet deserves oblivion. It is more difficult than perhaps we think to ruin a land beyond all healing (though the Soviet Union did its dreadful best): elsewhere in Tolkien's epic – which has played a part in reawakening love of the living earth – living creatures stubbornly resist dominion and exclusion. But there are steps towards that waste and desolation, and steps away. Peoples may begin to repair the ruins (not by tidying them up, but instead by letting in the jungle[31]). Peoples who wholly ruin 'their' land can no more claim a right to do so than to ruin their children. In the network of national and supranational republics, it will be a people's nearest neighbours that should support or rebuke them. What is done upstream affects downstreamers; what is done at the shore affects the mountains. It is right and proper that families should rear children, and nations care for lands; but precisely because it is, our neighbours cannot leave us alone to make a complete hash of it.

So one step away from Mordor is a local and historically minded love of the land wherein we find ourselves and others. To destroy its elements, to break up its network of relationships for personal or immediate profit is to initiate changes that may prove catastrophic (as they will in the tropical rain-forests) and will certainly bring loss as well as gain. 'There is no sense and no sanity in objecting to the desecration of the flag while tolerating and justifying as a daily business the desecration of the country for which it stands.'[32] It does not follow that all change should be resisted: the contrary of Mordor is Lothlorien, where there is no decay and memory is kept keen for ever – but that is no home for mortals. In Tolkien's fable it must either pass into the Utter West or be transformed into another version of the Dark. Refusal of all change is, in the end, exactly the same sin, the lust to have things all our way. Fangorn *might* have plotted, like a greater Willowman, 'to cover all the world with [his] trees and choke all other living things'.[33] Success in such a plot would not be very different from Sauron's, and would end in the same place.

Loving the land we live in, in a proper way, involves respecting the variety of things and working with them to achieve a life that never simply stops. To live in harmony is to allow for many tunes and instruments: not to let the brass predominate nor yet exclude them altogether; neither to poison all the violinists nor refuse to admit the possibility of computer keyboards. That image, of course, assumes that we have some conception of an orchestra, and its symphony. It even half-encourages the misleading thought that we are the conductors. Both thoughts have their dangers. The second, which marches with the fashionable cant of 'stewardship', I will address in a later chapter. The former leads me back to this chapter's problem.

We can form a partial image of sound national, local care. A people embedded in their land, acquainted with its vagaries and on speaking terms with its inhabitants, have some chance of looking after it. They may fall into error by refusing change and immigration. They may fail by seeking to impose their own changed ways on something that is not just theirs. Seeking to protect the land we may encourage local care, the 'rights' of indigenous peoples against invasion. I should add that a recent Green Party conference, considering a motion on behalf of indigenous peoples, was told that 'this would play into the hands of the shire Tories'. The answer came at once that 'shire Tories are not indigenous peoples' – a fine example of stereotypes at work, but also a hint of what is needed. We easily deny that 'shire Tories' need protection against invasive experimentation on the land they live in because we think that they have power enough already, that they are not embedded in the land but probably in the City, that they or their ancestors were themselves invaders or despoilers, that they are not people we can patronize or love. Amazonian Indians, by contrast, have no power, are utterly dependent on and not destructive of their land, and can be used – until they begin to object – as pretexts for our wish to dominate. Those who would defend the indigenes are sometimes seen – by those same indigenes – as not unlike the resettlers and despoilers that they react against.

Good nationalists are ones who do not claim too much, and who are ready to allow on the global level that diversity and gradual change that is a necessity within their neighbourhood. There is perhaps no easy rule: it is most probably an error to introduce new kinds of tree or animals, because we cannot know their effects (which may include a wildfire spread of the new kind, to the detriment of all existing kinds); it is an equivalent error to despise the maple tree or rabbit just because they happened to reach these shores mere hundreds of years, and not millennia, ago. As Aristotle showed us, it is easier to know what's wrong than what is right, and where we place the mark in any given case depends on our deep-seated attitudes. What sort of world is this? What is our place in it?

## D Living in the world, or out of it

The National Socialists and many other thinkers of the day absorbed a post-Darwinian synthesis. Diverse nations were good things because they provided the material for evolutionary selection. Nature 'tried out' different kinds, and every one was programmed to do its utmost to survive: anything less would be to betray the Earth. It is of course some comfort that the Nazis lost, and were, therefore, by their standards, proven wrong. Each individual, each kind, each nation is driven to maintain itself and grow, and 'progress' occurs in consequence. On the one hand friends are only allies of convenience, to be betrayed; on the other, each individual, at whatever level, is made up of lesser individuals who sacrifice their little selves to support the whole. We do not exist as 'entities', so Thomas says,[34] or not at any rate as strict substances, indivisible and self-sufficient. It may surprise you that Descartes, so often and so vigorously condemned by modern ecomystics, said the same.

> Though each of us is a person distinct from others whose interests are accordingly in some way different from those of the rest of the world, we must still think that none of us could subsist alone and each one of us is really one of the many parts of the universe, and more particularly a part of the earth, the state, the society, the family to which we belong by our domicile, our oath of allegiance and our birth.[35]

If we were to grant that individuals are fundamentally antagonistic then the existence of larger, compound individuals is explicable only by the domination of lesser selves, absorbed into the being of the leader. If we begin instead from the bare fact of compound individuals, every being to maintain its own must maintain a myriad others 'inside' and 'outside' itself. Dominion and synergy are two basic forms of being-with the land. Jeffers again, condemning us through the mouth of a rural mystic:

> They have done what never was done before, not as a people takes a land to love it and be fed,
> A little, according to need and love, and again a little; sparing the country tribes, mixing
> Their blood with theirs, their minds with all the rocks and rivers, their flesh with the soil.[36]

Jeffers here allows his character, and maybe he himself believed, the fantasy that somewhere, far away and long ago, people lived gently with the land, not wanting more. This may be so. Much longer ago prokaryotes and mitochondria worked together to be eukaryotes, and single cells invented many-celled beings like us. Neither invention seems to require dominion. Maybe hives do, although it is not clear just who is dominating whom: the perception that queens dominate can be revised by the discovery that it is her sisters who've selected her to carry on their line (since insects resemble their aunts more than their mothers). It is at least not obvious that human communities, including their community with land, just have to be dominions. There are other forms, even if ones that are not fully realized in the world of present experience.

Similarly, if we begin from the unhuman universe and seek to blend our minds with that, learning to praise absorption in the land and to conceive us as we first conceived wild or domestic animals, or bacterial infections, we seem to end in ignorant and self-defensive hordes. But if we start from the other end, from actual and historical experience of a land imbued with memories, we may come to conceive of the one world of which our history is a fragment. Evolutionary history can be conceived far more as a co-operative enterprise than a competitive, though I shall have more to say in a later chapter about the proper interpretation of current theory.

What then of those without a land, or those whose land is only a far-off dream or destiny? By this I do not mean city-dwellers. There is no need to feed the delusion that cities are not part of nature. 'There is', as Chesterton said in his introduction to a 1920s work on rural Europe, 'something fantastic about the very phrase "Back to the Land", as if we were at present walking about on the clouds or the sea. . . . Our urban populations have actually forgotten that we all live on the land.'[37] But there are people much like Kipling's Cat and unlike any real cat known to me, to whom all places are alike. These too may go two ways. There are some intellectuals or politicians, maybe, who do not think they have a natural home, who do not notice where their water comes from, who move from carefully identical hotel to hotel. The rest of us are usually aware that this contrived cosmopolitanism is unreal, that the would-be world-citizens are products and dependants of a very precise historical and biological niche, that they are would-be dominators. Chesterton understood the Crusades as a defence of the mystery of locality, incarnation, art against 'a devouring giant out of the deserts to whom all places were the same', 'a quarrel between one man who wanted [Jerusalem] and another man who could not see why it was wanted'.[38] He was probably wrong about Islam: the Prophet spoke in favour of the love of place,[39] and there are holy places for all Islamic traditions, but he was perhaps right to notice that Islam was a form of universal religion, civilized values, that must make loyalty to any particular nation (even the Arab nation) dubious. Time brings its revenges: it is now the imperial West that looks like the devouring giant to whom all places are the same – and who will make them all the same if she has her way. But 'citizen of the world' once had another meaning: Cynics and Stoics alike sought to transcend their local habitations, not in contempt of them, but out of love for the whole world of humans, gods, animals and vegetation gathering itself together over time. We are citizens of the world-city when we acknowledge that we share it with our friends, that all of us stand under the one law. We do what nature, or God, requires of us when we seek not to dominate but share. 'The moral consequence of faith in God', so Niebuhr tells us,

> is the universal love of all being in Him. . . . This is [faith's] requirement: that all beings, not only our friends, but also our enemies, not only men but also animals and the inanimate, be met with reverence, for all are friends in the friendship of the one to whom we are reconciled in faith.[40]

We need, within the nation, people that remain open to a transcendent vocation, who can be reminded of those people, creatures, things that have no standing in the nearby, closed-off, national universe.

> If one were to write that Jews have always been in the forefront of movements designed to liberate the poor and oppressed, that they have always taken up the cudgels on behalf of trade unionists, idealistic internationalists and victims of superstition, one would be saying, objectively, exactly what the *völkisch* writers of the 1920s were saying.[41]

That is, I remark in passing, the only final justification of a true university, which

> takes its place alongside church and state and other communities or institutions without subordination to anyone of these. It is as directly responsible to the transcendence in the performance of its particular duties of study and teaching as they are in the administration of the laws or in their preaching and worship.[42]

It was, correspondingly, Heidegger's sin to subordinate the academy to the Führer as the pure expression of a national purpose, and the sin of far too many academics to provide the skills for a short-sighted and destructive 'agribusiness'. 'Located in a nation [a university] is not of the nation but of the universe; though it is part of a culture, it cannot but try to transcend the outlook of that culture.' I hope I need not remind you that this is very far from the strategy of 'deracinated intellectuals' all too fixed in their socioeconomic class. Niebuhr's academics aim to root themselves in the eternal, but are supported in the endeavour by the culture that surrounds them.

But that is to anticipate a later discussion: here I should only identify a form of 'cosmopolitanism' that requires us to respect all lesser organisms and communities within the living globe. All wanton killing, and ecological warfare, is forbidden by Islamic law.

> In a celebrated address to the first Syrian expedition Abu Bakr the first Caliph said 'Stop O people, that I may give you ten rules to keep by heart! Do not commit treachery, nor depart from the right path. You must not mutilate, neither kill a child or aged man or woman. Do not destroy a palm tree, nor burn it with fire and do not cut down any fruitful tree. You must not slay any of the flock or the herds or the camels, save for your sustenance.'[43]

On the other hand, the Prophet set fire to the palm trees of Banu Nadir, and the Koran reads 'whatever palm-trees you cut down or leave standing upon their roots, that was by God's leave and that he might degrade the ungodly'.[44] There is clearly some room for dispute even amongst honest and honourable universalists. The other form, despised and feared by nationalists, refuses to give due honour to the gods of place, and hardly notices what it destroys. Conversely: a decent nationalism honours the gods of other places than its own, and does not seek to become an empire of whatever kind. Indecent nationalism, despised and feared by universalists, is ready to destroy whatever it sees as rivals.

Hitler claimed to respect animals, and so perhaps he did. But that attempt, or multiple attempts, to provide the 'new religion' that we need was deeply flawed by its despair of humane values, by its preference for dominating models of co-operative being, and by its disregard of individuals. Environmentalists who wish us to wake up had better take more care. 'It is deep peace', no doubt, 'and final joy

> To know that the great world lives, whether man dies or not. The beauty of things is not harnessed to human
> Eyes and the little active minds: it is absolute.[45]

That was something like Aristotle's view as well, who identified the highest human life as one devoted to the contemplation of a world in which human beings were not the highest form of life.[46] But if that absolute beauty, that great world, is one where entities are antagonists, and larger wholes are only formed by sacrifice and war, then waking up to it reveals our dreams of justice and of friendship as just dreams. If that beauty is expressed in death, decay, extinction, then human predators are no more than its agents, who may expect a like reward.

There are three options open to us. Either we deny all dualism and bind ourselves to act as natural beings in a world of war; or else we insist that human beings must be for ever different, must somehow 'defy' the workings of the world-machine; or else we claim to find out the real world through our experience of loving community. The second position, though it is defended by liberal-minded biologists like Richard Dawkins, seems quite absurd. Either the world is war, or else the Jewish dream and demand for justice, 'when they shall not hurt or destroy in all [God's] holy mountain', is someday to be vindicated. 'True eschatology is a dream life about a better future.'[47] To blame the Jews for ecological crisis is exactly the wrong move. It is, on the contrary, the Jewish dream alone that lends us hope.

## Notes

1. R. Jeffers, 'An Extinct Vertebrate' in *What Odd Expedients, and Other Poems*, ed. R. I. Scott (Archon Books: Hamden, CT, 1981), p. 54.

2. Compare Logan Pearsall Smith: 'I like my universe as immense, grim, icy and pitiless as possible': *All Trivia* (Constable & Co.: London, 1933), p. 154.

3. B. Russell, cited by Scott in Jeffers, *What Odd Expedients*, p. 6, from R. G. Egner, *Russell's Best: Silhouettes in Satire* (Allen & Unwin: London, 1958), p. 30.

4. S. Weil, *Notebooks*, tr. A. Wills (Routledge & Kegan Paul: London, 1956), vol. II, p. 423.

5. R. Jeffers, *The Double Axe and Other Poems* (Liveright: New York, 1977), pp. 145f.

6. R. C. Zaehner, *Our Savage God* (Collins: Glasgow, 1974).

7. C. Spretnak and F. Capra, *Green Politics* (Paladin: London, 1985), p. 127; see A. Bramwell, *Ecology in the Twentieth Century* (Yale University Press: New Haven, 1989).

8. R. A. Pois, *National Socialism and the Religion of Nature* (St Martin's Press: New York, 1986), p. 58.

9. E. Krieck (1936); cited by Pois, *National Socialism*, p. 117.

10. W. H. Auden, 'Memorial for the City' in *Collected Shorter Poems 1927–57* (Faber: London, 1966), p. 289.

11. F. Kersten, *The Kersten Memoirs 1940–5*, tr. C. Fitzgibbons and J. Oliver (Macmillan: London, 1956), pp. 115f.; see Pois, *National Socialism*, p. 34.

12. C. Burt, 'The trend of national intelligence', *British Journal of Sociology* 1 (1950); cited by M. Canavan, *G. K. Chesterton: Radical Populist* (Harcourt Brace Jovanovich: New York and London, 1977), p. 58.

13. C. W. Armstrong; cited by Canavan, ibid., p. 67.

14. G. K. Chesterton, 'Ballade d'une Grande Dame', *Collected Poems* (Methuen: London, 1950), p. 190. It is uncomfortably, and ironically, true that Chesterton did often blame the Jews (that is, cynical financiers) for these theories; he did, before his end, speak out for them.

15. Pois, *National Socialism*, p. 132.

16. J. B. Callicott, *In Defense of the Land Ethic* (State University of New York Press: Albany, 1989), p. 30. Callicott does go on to deplore such a mechanization of living things, but not, so far as I can tell, because they are thereby injured.

17. See A. Dobson, *Green Political Thought* (Unwin Hyman: London, 1990), pp. 64, 94.

18. A. Toynbee and D. Ikeda, *Choose Life* (Oxford University Press: London, 1976), p. 324.

19. O. Patterson, *Ethnic Chauvinism* (Stein & Day: New York, 1977), p. 151.

20. W. Blake, *Complete Writings*, ed. G. Keynes (Clarendon Press: Oxford, 1966), p. 151.

21. F. Roosevelt (1937); cited by J. Hart, *The Spirit of the Earth* (Paulist Press: New Jersey, 1984), p. 15.

22. T. Jefferson; cited by A. Koch, *Power, Morals and the Founding Fathers* (Cornell University Press: Ithaca, 1961), p. 28.

23. T. Jefferson (1816); cited by A. Koch, *The Philosophy of Thomas Jefferson* (Columbia University Press: New York, 1943), p. 163.

24. G. K. Chesterton, *The Outline of Sanity* (1926), p. 11; cited by Canavan, *G. K. Chesterton*, p. 83.

25. K. Sale, *Dwellers in the Land* (Sierra Club: Washington, DC, 1985).

26. K. Lynch, *What Time Is This Place?* (MIT Press: Cambridge, MA, 1972), pp. 41, 126.

27. Psalm 137.1, 4 (BCP).

28. Dobson, *Green Political Thought*, p. 121.

29. 'Much of the British countryside, with this "traditional" patchwork of pastures, woodland coppices, hedgerows, and heathland, is the product of many generations of developing agricultural techniques and land-holding traditions – sometimes interspersed with periods of relatively rapid change, like that of the enclosures': Department of the Environment, *Reply to First Report from Environmental Committee* (May 1985), p. 3; cited by R. Attfield and C. Dell (eds), *Values, Conflict and the Environment* (Ian Ramsey Centre: Oxford, 1989), p. 5.

30. J. R. R. Tolkien, *The Lord of the Rings* (Allen & Unwin: London, 1966, 2nd edn), vol. II, p. 251.

31. See M. F. Smith, 'Letting in the jungle', *Journal of Applied Philosophy* 8 (1991), pp. 145–54.

32. W. Berry, *What Are People For?* (Rider Books: London, 1990), p. 127.

33. Tolkien, *The Lord of the Rings*, vol. II, p. 200.

34. L. Thomas, *The Lives of a Cell* (Penguin: Harmondsworth, 1978), p. 53.

35. R. Descartes, *Philosophical Letters*, ed. A. Kenny (Clarendon Press: Oxford, 1970), p. 172 (15 September 1645).

36. R. Jeffers, 'A Redeemer' in *Selected Poetry* (Random House: New York, 1933), p. 189.

37. G. K. Chesterton, Introduction in H. D. Irvine, *Making of Rural Europe* (Allen & Unwin: London, 1923), p. 7.

38. G. K. Chesterton, *Short History of England* (Chatto & Windus: London, 1917), pp. 64f.

39. See H. Enayat, *Modern Islamic Political Thought* (Macmillan: London, 1982), p. 112.

40. H. Richard Niebuhr, *Radical Monotheism and Western Culture* (Harper & Brothers: New York, 1960), p. 126.

41. A. Bramwell, *Blood and Soil: Richard Walther Darré and Hitler's 'Green Party'* (Kensal Press: Bourne End, 1985), p. 36.

42. H. Niebuhr, *Radical Monotheism*, p. 96.

43. Cited by M. Khadduri, *War and Peace in the Law of Islam* (Johns Hopkins Press: Baltimore, 1955), p. 102. The remaining rules are: 'You are likely to pass by people who devoted their lives to monastic service; leave them to that to which they have devoted their lives. You are likely, likewise, to find people who will present to you meals of many kinds. You may eat; but do not forget to mention the name of Allah.'

44. Koran 59.5: A. J. Arberry (tr.), *The Koran* (World's Classics, OUP, 1964), p. 673. There is a tendency for Muslims to reckon that the ungodly are fair game: there is an identical tendency, of course, amongst the inheritors of Christendom.

45. Jeffers, *The Double Axe*, p. 113.

46. See my 'The better part' in A. Phillips Griffiths (ed.), *Philosophy and Ethics* (CUP, forthcoming).

47. M. Fox, *Creation Spirituality* (Harper: San Francisco, 1990), p. 113.

......................................4

# The liberation of life

.........................................

## A  On not blaming Plato

Those environmentalists who do not blame the Jews often prefer to
blame the Greeks instead. I will confess that there are elements of
great Greek thought that I wish had not been absorbed by Christian
thinkers, and then bequeathed to post-Christian humanists, notably
the Stoic disdain for beasts. It is of course absurd to blame this
on 'the Greeks', as though Greek thinkers never criticized the view
that beasts lacked any moral standing. And even Stoic thinkers also
provided an account of moral development, from parental affection
and friendship, considerably more in tune with evolutionary thought
than recent contract-theorists have ever managed.[1] The status of individual animals and duties of forbearance and benevolence toward
them are not, however, what is at issue here. Greek thought was
deeply damaging, we are told, because it drew a distinction between
the changeful material world and the transcendent and eternal one.
'We have largely assimilated the view of the ancient Greeks that all
physical matter is corrupt because it is subject to decay and that only
the purely spiritual is good.'[2] To which I must respond, what ancient
Greeks, and who are we? McDonagh, in a rather better book, is
only a little more exact, blaming our crisis on Cartesian, Gnostic or
Neoplatonic revulsion 'at the thought of humankind being firmly

rooted in the earth'.[3] 'Gnostic' covers so much ground and means so little that this may be true, but neither Cartesians nor Platonists (who disagree on almost everything) give any evidence of this revulsion. In theological circles nowadays 'Platonic' is pejorative, and 'Cartesian' as bad. I am no Cartesian myself, though I often find myself defending Descartes against intemperate attack. Matthew Fox declares that 'Creation spirituality takes opposite positions on just about all of Descartes' basic principles' – and wholly misrepresents the latter.[4] Maybe it is true that our existence depends upon the earth's (as Fox says: 'Earth exists and therefore we are'), but that has nothing at all to do with Descartes' proof that he does exist (because he cannot deny that he is thinking). I have already cited Descartes' declaration that we exist as dependent, partial entities. I must add that he also emphasizes that we are not angels (nor ghosts) in a machine. 'If an angel were in a human body he would not have sensations as we do, but would simply perceive the motions which are caused by external objects and in this way would differ from a real man.'[5] Nor does he insist on believing only what can, to us, make perfect sense: if we have reason to believe that we are thinking things, and also bodily, it hardly matters that we cannot make sense of their connection, 'because to do so it is necessary to conceive them as a single thing and at the same time to conceive them as two things, which is self-contradictory'.[6] We turn out to be bodily beings, even if our bodies have to be distinguished, in thought, from our thinking selves. It is very rash of any Christian, and any environmentalist, to deny that we are conscious. If we are not, then there are no minds to mind about, nor any minds to mind. I have yet to be convinced that Descartes was environmentally pernicious (though he, and his followers, were very bad for animals). Fashionable contempt for anything that can be labelled 'Cartesian' dualism seems much more likely to have very bad effects (on which more hereafter). That Plato was pernicious, or Platonism, seems to me just wrong.

But what is it that theologians, and environmentalists, decry? The Greek, or at least the Platonic, view is said to be that this world is imperfect, that what should be is not entirely what here seems to be, that what is here is so far shifting, relative and defective as hardly to be describable at all, that there is nonetheless a real world that we can reasonably hope to learn about. Is this not true? Must we instead believe that the world is obvious to simple sense, that there is no truth beyond what appears to us, that what is here is just what should be here? In that case, what are we troubled about? There is no crisis, since what should be is no different from what is. There is no crisis, for nothing different or unobvious will ever happen. There is no crisis, for most people still don't see there is. There is no crisis, for anyone can give an exact and simple account of any little problem and devise a response if any seems to be needed. If Platonism is as obviously false as some theologians say, then so is all environmentalism.

Of course there is more to Platonism than that, but what is it that is so obviously false, so obviously to blame for our alleged neglect of the material universe? Plato would perhaps be surprised to learn that we neglect it: he might argue, on the contrary, that we esteem material value, what we can physically possess, above the values that he pointed to. Romantics say that primitives, so-called, mind more about what they are than what they own: if so, they are good Platonists. It is at least as easy, indeed, to depict Black Elk as Platonist as to show that he was environmentally aware. Black Elk, I should explain, was an Oglala Sioux shaman, whose life-story was recorded by John G. Neihardt.[7] Those who use his story to prove that Native Americans were environmentally friendly do him a considerable injustice. First of all, he was a Sioux, not one of a homogeneous population of 'Amerindians'. Second, it is quite clear that he was deeply unusual in his own nation: from the age of nine he regretted the killing of other creatures – except those who murdered his people – and wished to be 'a relative to all that is'.[8] One might as well argue that Europeans (from Iceland to the Ukraine) are environmentally friendly on the basis of the reminiscences of Henry Salt, or St Kieran.

But let us agree that public policy has all too often been founded in the easy assumption that matter is but material. Matter is the unformed, whether we thereby speak of primeval chaos, or stones that have not yet been carved or built, or trees that have not yet been turned to timber, or dogs not yet domesticated, or savage peoples not yet civilized (which is, tamed). Each of those things save chaos does have some form or other, but is counted as material for a further ordering form. Value accrues to things by how far they are formed, how far they have been disciplined and changed to serve a higher good. Sometimes the material is recalcitrant, sometimes it yearns to be fulfilled, but either way only the formed thing has much value, and that only so far as it serves the good. Public policy also equates that good with states of human consciousness. So nothing at all is valuable except what promotes those states called human happiness. Why these are good it is impolite to ask. In so far as some things serve human happiness more directly or intensely there is a sort of hierarchy of value. Plants are for animals; animals are for human beings; women are for men; labourers and farmers for the ruling classes.

All that was, perhaps, a fair enough description of public policy, not only in the West, though some of its elements are perhaps defunct. But I have two objections to the argument. First, the story does not seem to me to be Platonic. Plato himself would perhaps have agreed with bits of it, but so would many other people. Of Plato's distinctive doctrines I see little sign. Second, the very same environmentalists who reject what they call Platonism seem to endorse the story as their own: if humankind is the apex or the 'growing tip' of evolution, and our goal to 'humanize' the world, how does that differ from our present policies?

It is first very strange that Platonists (or Stoics or any Greek philosophers) should be attacked for being anthropocentric. On the contrary, they put the cosmos first, and gave humans honour in so far as they saw and served the beauty of the whole. That we are not the most important things in the world is not, as McKibben suggests,[9] a *new* idea: it is what tradition says. 'The world does not exist for the sake of man, but man exists for its sake.'[10] The sin of wanting more, *pleonexia*, is what Greek moralists are always on about. It could be argued that without clear revelation of what needs the cosmos has it will be hard not to slip into serving just our human needs. It is all too easy, even if absurd, to argue that human beings have the one merit that they *can* see that other things matter more than they do, and that therefore nothing matters more than them. But this is ordinary self-deceit, not Platonism nor philosophy.

Let me attempt again to grasp the charge. Maybe Plato and his successors did not intend to say that human happiness was all, and that all other things could only at best have instrumental value. Indeed he could not have intended this, since he expressly denies that the good is fixed by what we happen to feel like. Either happiness is not all that matters, or it is not happiness unless it accurately prefers the good. But isn't the analysis of form and matter, and of a hierarchy of value and existence a Platonic one? Being and Value alike depend on form, and therefore on external discipline. In so far as things here-now are never wholly formed, they do no more than remind us of true value. In one way things here-now are better if they are formed; in another nothing here-now is valuable in itself. The birds we once called dodos were never quite what dodos should be, and all a dodo should be is eternal fact: nothing of value can be lost, for only eternal truths are values, and the changing world never does more than remind us of what we know. Socrates as well maybe embodied philosophical beauty, or maybe begat his immortality on eternal beauty: the historical and changing individual had value only in that he almost showed that beauty, and nothing of value has been lost by his execution.

I still have two objections. First, anti-Platonic theologians will also claim that God remembers everything of value, that no value can be lost forever. There may be a difference between those who think the Dodo is eternal in God's Idea of the World, and those who think God only remembers dodos (being Himself as temporal a being as any). Indeed there is, and mostly to the discredit of the latter, but the one view seems no more environmentally pernicious than the other. In so far as theological dogma is a coded proposal about what we should do, rather than (wholly or significantly) a report about what is the case, the two versions seem very nearly identical. We should not, and need not, hang on to particular tokens of any ideal type, for fear that their like will never be seen again. Because the form is eternal we can put up with the change. Because it is always more than any particular example we can expect to find new aspects of it over time. If 'Beauty' were only what we have so far seen as beautiful, worship would be the kind of conservatism beloved of bureaucrats: that nothing be allowed to change. It is because Platonism does not equate Beauty with particular beauties that we can be reassured: change need not be an evil, because Beauty is realized in indefinitely (infinitely?) many ways.

> All things counter, original, spare, strange;
> Whatever is fickle, freckled (who knows how?)
> With swift, slow; sweet, sour; adazzle, dim;
> He fathers-forth whose beauty is past change:
> Praise him.[11]

The alternative version has a similar moral: if that is satisfactory, so is Platonism. That there are after all real losses is a complex thought I must defer, and that individuals as such may not be well understood as simple tokens of a type: neither thought is easy, and neither is any better handled by the sort of self-consciously anti-Platonic theory that I am here reviewing.

Secondly, Plato would not consent to crude dichotomies. We may say that a sculptor imposes form on unformed marble, but there is no need to resort to Inuits, as Harré does, to find a different model.[12] Platonists, from the Church Fathers to Leibniz, speak instead of the sculptor's releasing the hidden form from matter. Formed things emerge by inner tendency as much as by external fiat. There is not first an unformed mass which is then licked to shape, as the bestiaries said that bear-cubs were. There is nothing that is unformed (which is why 'prime matter' as the bare substrate of change is very nearly nothing), and when formed things change their appearance it reveals what was there already. Living things have their formal principle in them; made things are the extension of another's form. A timber house is not a better thing than a tree, though it is more of a thing, an entity, than a pile of timber is. Things exist at all in so far as there is an approximation to what things of that kind should be. That they should be like that is an eternal truth if it is a truth at all. To be is to be something, to embody some real type, some standard of being. 'Everything that lives is holy' is a genuinely Platonic thought. In so far as something has defects it begins to lose its grip on being at all, but absolute corruption is impossible: what is literally nothing, does not exist.

So Plato's analysis does not present us with a hierarchy of extrinsic values, nor can we infer from it that material things are valuable only instrumentally. On the contrary, everything that exists at all partly embodies a particular value. Why it is that the Good requires these things to be in these so various ways is not a question that Plato even attempts to answer. If the Seventh Letter is genuine he said that could not be conveyed by reasoned argument, but only seen. What must be because it is good that it should be, is not merely us. There is therefore no good reason to suppose that everything exists to do us good, in any straightforward sense. We will be better for seeing the good reflected in the world, but its goodness does not reside in making us better. In seeing that different things are better or worse according to their kinds we see what is the case whether we see it or not. The plain before Mordor was not as it should be.

But surely we 'know' that Plato despised the body, that his greatest pagan successor, Plotinus, 'seemed ashamed' to have a body at all? Surely we know that Plato placed the greatest value in exercising intellect? Must that not count against any Platonic basis for concern for the world, and for certainly non-intellectual creatures? It is clearly true that policy-makers are not Platonists, but did not the Platonic heritage coax Christendom, and therefore the post-Christian state, to think that temporal concerns don't matter, that material being is no more, at best, than an egg, a nest, a mother to be abandoned? If we wish now to awaken to a religious, binding consciousness of a sacred earth we must purge Christendom of Plato's ghost. We must sing hymns to Holy Matter, and learn to love the changeful, mortal world.

The difficulty remains that we dare not slip into mere pantheism. There must be a distinction between what is and ought to be, or else we lose all right to complain about global warming, deforestation, desertification, the poisoning of habitats and the death of kinds. Pure pantheists must welcome all of that, as well as nuclear spasm if that should be. Nor, having abandoned Plato, can we easily insist that something is imperfect just because it ends. That may seem right enough: as Aristotle said, things aren't improved merely by adding that they last forever! And we might reasonably infer that nothing is made worse just because it doesn't. Isn't the fact of briefness and mortality what adds an unbearable beauty to the things we love? No one should wish the thing she loves eternal, for it would then lose the nature that she loves. I don't agree with this myself, and neither should environmentalists: why not, if that is so, accept the briefness of species and their habitats? Doesn't the real prospect of extinction intensify our love of the living earth, if it intensifies our love of human individuals to know they die? Environmentalists as much as Platonists must wish that nothing of what they love is lost. It is true enough, as the carol says, that 'times do shift, thus times do shift; each thing its place doth hold; new things succeed, new things succeed, as former things grow old'. Or as Marcus Aurelius declared: the world is in love with creating, and so I shall love it too. But the new things cannot, must not, wholly erase the old. If we loved only what was new we could not even create, any more than one who acknowledges no debt to the past can even commit her future.

So what is at issue here? The merely historical question, whether Plato or the Platonists despised the physical universe or urged us to exploit it for our transitory gain is easily answered. They did not. Plato's imagined healthy city is self-sufficient, growing what it needs and needing nothing except what nature gives. The wish to have more, and fear of others across a border who want more, creates a luxuriating city that must defend and discipline itself or die. The city in remission which is popularly called Plato's Republic is an attempt to achieve simplicity under the guidance of experienced rulers who will not put their private interests before those of their people, and who have somehow seen how the great world images or partly embodies the good. It sounds, in fact, not altogether unlike Wendell Berry's dream:

> We need a system of decentralized, small-scale industries to transform the products of our fields and woodlands and streams: small creameries, cheese factories, canneries, grain mills, saw mills, furniture factories, and the like. By 'small' I mean simply a size that would not be destructive of the appearance, the health and the quiet of the countryside.[13]

In *The Laws* Plato further insists that the citizens of his suggested city must revere the earth, and the gods of place, as well as justice: 'The land is [our] ancestral home and [we] must cherish it even more than children cherish their mother; furthermore, the Earth is a goddess and mistress of mortal men, and the gods and spirits already established in the locality must be treated with the same respect.'[14]

That earliest city, by the way, is vegetarian, and it was the Platonists who long maintained an attention to the welfare of our non-human kin. Dividing the world into humankind and everything else, human and non-human, is, on Plato's explicit word, a false dichotomy.[15] Until this century the only writing by a 'professional philosopher' on our duties to and about the non-human that actually defended them was by the Neoplatonist Porphyry. Porphyry's great master, Plotinus, was perhaps 'ashamed' that he was still condemned to partial views, that he had desires and needs that troubled his tranquillity: it does not follow that he despised the world. Quite otherwise: he devoted one whole diatribe to the refutation of those who thought our world was the creation of a lesser, misled godling. Fox's judgement is that Plotinus' recommendations 'leave out delight and pleasure, creativity and justice; their goal is not compassion but contemplation and the turning away from the earth and all that relates to it'.[16] I cannot imagine what evidence he has for this. On the contrary, Plotinus was entrusted with the care of orphan (and other) children, gave advice to the then emperor, saved Porphyry from melancholic suicide, and wrote with unprecedented brilliance about the beauty of justice. True beauty, for Plotinus, lies in life, that marvellous, seemingly chaotic tangle that has – for us – its being over time. The patterns of the Mandelbrot set strike us as enthrallingly beautiful precisely because they are infinitely various, and always new, and yet identifiably the same.

> For why is there more light of beauty on a living face and only a trace of it on a dead one, even if its flesh and proportions are not yet wasted away? And are not

statues more beautiful if they are more lifelike, even if others are better pro-
portioned; and is not an ugly living man more beautiful than a beautiful statue?[17]

That moral approbation comes under the same heading is a thought
that has been out of fashion for many years.[18] We have so far forgotten our past as to imagine that calling a character beautiful is only a
strained metaphor. But we can at least understand what Plotinus
means, even if we do not altogether agree with him:

> As it is not for those to speak of the graceful forms of the material world who have
> never seen them or known their grace – men born blind, let us suppose – in the
> same way those must be silent upon the beauty of noble conduct and of learning
> and all that order who have never cared for such things, nor may those tell of the
> splendour of virtue who have never known the face of Justice and of Moral
> Wisdom beautiful beyond the beauty of Evening and Dawn. Such vision is for
> those only who see with the Soul's sight – and at the vision they will rejoice, and
> awe will fall upon them and a trouble deeper than all the rest could ever stir, for
> now they are moving in the realm of Truth. This is the spirit that Beauty must ever
> induce, wonderment and a delicious trouble, longing and love and a trembling
> that is all delight.[19]

The beauty of the world is real, and the attentive love required of us
includes a real concern for all our fellow mortals. In those days of
course the great world seemed inexhaustible. How could we do Gaia
any harm? But there were local cases to be regretted: the deforestation and erosion of Attica was well advanced by Plato's day
(though this observation did not have quite the resonance we now
impute to it). Greed, pride and anger, the wish to have things
now and on our terms, were sins that could and would destroy the
local basis of our life together. Cities would fall, and civilizations,
because we forgot that we were part of the world's cycles, forgot to
take account of what, materially, is needed for our life. All this makes
it absurd to blame Plato; as absurd indeed as it is to blame the human
authors of the Torah, who required that we not seize everything as
ours, that we leave land for the wild things and the land fallow every
seventh and fiftieth year. It is especially absurd when we recall that
currently remembered heroines and heroes of the ecomystical like
Hildegard of Bingen, or the Romantic poets, were Platonists (i.e., the
very people Matthew Fox acclaims)!

## B Worrying about the absolute

I am examining, remember, different 'religious' answers to our environmental crisis. It is understandable that many of these are partly defined by their opposition to what went before. If older, established ideologies have got us where we are, we might as well try something different. This assumption fits too well with other, established habits of mind to be easily resisted. Every new idea must distance itself from older ones because it is 'obvious' that older ideologues were fools or knaves. Because the modern scientific movement, and much of the philosophical, formed itself in opposition to 'Aristotle', or 'scholasticism', or 'the Church', good moderns now repeat those seventeenth-century gibes without ever thinking it necessary to check the facts. People repeat the gibes even if a later fashion has also led them to express contempt (without ever troubling to read them) for the very philosophers and scientists who first coined the gibes! The image especially of Aristotle amongst working scientists (even those who actually reproduce his ideas) is unrecognizable as Aristotle to any Aristotelian scholar. The image of Plato amongst many modern theologians (which class includes many who are not Christians, or even believing theists) is almost as absurd.

But even if environmentalists and others are quite wrong in what they think of Plato, or the ancient world in general, they may be right, or at least worth listening to, in what they say on their own behalf. Our crisis partly stems from deliberate inattention to the living earth, and this in turn from the conviction that 'we' don't belong on earth and that what is supremely valuable is forever beyond the reach of any harm. The various religious answers that I have so far explored agree in thinking that we ought to remember our terrestrial being, that we ought to allow our affections, and attention, to be engaged by little local entities, within a larger, struggling whole. Reality – the reality by which we should be engaged – is not an abstract diagram, to be learned through higher mathematics. We are not ghosts in a machine that operates in perfect obedience to natural law. We cannot be sure what actually will happen, in experienced detail, merely by identifying known factors and performing abstract calculations. Our epistemology must be far more tentative, more alert to accumulated detail, more alive to the values identified in loving attention to individuals. Our ontology must emphasize those same individuals, never reducible to tokens of ideal types, and recognize that they exist, essentially, in time. Reality is always changing, and true knowledge must change with it. Reality is always particular, and true knowledge must be of those individuals. This is why ecofeminists and nationalists alike have, after all, a sort of case. As long as we believe that the reality we should attend to is one entirely defined in abstract, universal terms, and the right method of attention is one stripped of all 'merely emotional' attachment, we may be distracted from the very things we need to care for in the everyday. The 'scholastic' God (even if it is actually very unlike the God described by mediaeval schoolmen) can usefully stand for a religious ideal that we should now disown. Any acceptable theism must speak in other terms, whether it is considered as a theory of How Things Are or only as a coded programme for how we should ourselves behave. This is why both 'process theology' and Teilhard de Chardin sometimes seem appropriate guides. My aim here, as elsewhere, is both to expound them with due sympathy, and to offer reasoned criticism. Both guides, I think, will prove to be from the army of King Oberon.

Modernist Christian theology comes in two forms. The softer sort endorses many of the old opinions (that there is a God, that Jesus is our saviour and liberal society, on the whole, a good), but strives to distance itself from metaphysical doctrine (that there is indeed a God, that Jesus is our Saviour and moral demands absolute). The harder kind declares itself agnostic or even atheistical about the doctrines, though somehow still suggesting that the Church was quite right in its day, and has preserved, poetically, many strange insights into human living. Process theologians are actually often far more metaphysically, dogmatically inclined, but the appeal of 'process theology' to sermonizers is that it suggests that *we* are all the God we know, that things have greatly improved since ancient times and that there is no absolute and menacing demand for which we need propitiation. We can, that is, feel hopeful even while we decline to endorse a genuinely prophetic promise. Is there any more respectable reason to take this model as seriously as some (mostly Christian) environmentalists have thought?

The 'scholastic' God is omnipotent, omniscient, omnipresent, eternal, impartial, self-sufficient, creator of all things, and impervious to change. Fortunately, it is also 'really' quite benevolent, although we could hardly have guessed this from the events it engineers. It follows that to be 'godlike' we must ourselves achieve some working resemblance to that grand ideal. Power and knowledge grow together; knowledge is achieved by moving toward the 'God's-eye', unperspectival view, and never changing one's mind; power is to be exercised impartially by one who needs as little as possible from anyone else. Feminists generally add that this ideal feeds on, and contributes to, the self-image favoured by aspiring males. Describing God as female, or in feminine modes, is an attempt to deconstruct those images, to offer a different ideal of selfhood and society while also attempting a different description of reality. Mediaeval schoolmen, of course, might well have denied that our job was to be 'god-like'. The very idea is ludicrous: it is God alone that can be God, and the very point of those obscure predicates is to emphasize what we can't be. If God is King it is possible to infer that kings are divine: but far more plausible to conclude that no man can be king, at least in the way he might prefer.[20] It is sometimes suggested that the Copernican (or Galilean) revolution was a humbling experience: suddenly we were a tiny part of an enormous universe, far off upon its margins. But any educated mediaeval knew that God was infinite, and that we had no chance – except by grace – of ever finding out what God had done, was doing in the vast expanses of creation. The revolution went the other way: suddenly we were no longer floundering in the mud of the very bottom, but flying aloft in heaven; suddenly it came to seem that the Mind of God (or as much of it as concerned physical reality) was present in us in the form of mathematics. Even in the face of this, philosophers continued to agree that we could not possibly expect to be 'self-sufficient, impervious to change, omnipotent or omniscient'. Being 'god-like', if we could manage it in any sense, would require us to be all-loving and a source of life: but our better bet would be to be obedient. 'What does the Lord require of you, but to do justly and to love mercy and to walk humbly with your God?'

But even if the Absolute God was not offered as an ideal for us to copy (which would have been absurd), perhaps it had a double, psychogenic effect? On the one hand (at least till Galileo recovered the Platonic dream) it made it clear that it would be ridiculous to struggle against Fate. Defying the Absolute is an occasional fantasy ('if God can send me to Hell for not adoring Him, to Hell I'll go'), but those who indulge it always seem to forget that such an Absolute controls their thoughts as well.

We can ravage the ecology, suppress the poor, murder prophets, adulterate the gospel, shake our fists defiantly at God and declare the world a mechanism and human beings machines. But the System of systems remains the ultimate arbiter, and we can no more secede from its jurisdiction than we can stop breathing air.[21]

I myself believe that this realization is, in the end, a humane and liberating one: but it can certainly be argued that such an irresistible Absolute denies us any power over 'our own' affairs, or the earth's future. Chernobyl (which is the star called Wormwood in the mythology of some readers of Revelation), the *Exxon Valdez*, the death of forests and the poisoning of the water tables are all divinely endorsed disasters, quite as much as the meteor that wiped away the dinosaurs (perhaps). The Absolute God may be benevolent, but even if it weren't we can do nothing at all against it. Give me a place to stand on and I will move the world, said Archimedes, exulting in his invention of the lever. But there is no place to stand on outside the Absolute, and so no way to move it.

The second psychological effect may be the Lucifer (or Oedipal) effect: admiration is often tinged with envy. The more we admire, or seem to admire, the more we resent the thing. We are glad when 'father-figures' and the like are shown for what we secretly hope they are; we aspire to replace them with a nobler, less corruptible embodiment of value. The desire to replace God may be grotesque – the more grotesque the larger the world turns out to be; the plan to replace 'Him' by becoming what we both love and hate is still more absurd. But the fact that dreams are fanciful does not make them unreal, or powerless. We secretly want to replace God, at least upon this globe, and think that we can do it by denying all connections to the rest of living creatures, by mimicking 'His' imperviousness, 'His' dominating power. One cure of all this nonsense might simply be to remind ourselves of who and what we are. Another – the one proposed for examination here – is to redescribe what God must be.

## C The divine relativity

The first thesis of the 'new philosophy' is that Western tradition has conceived the self, even the human self, as separate and absolute, and is thereby committed to the problem identified by Thomas Hobbes, the war of each against all. The welfare of my self, on this account, is separate from the welfare of any other thing, and may require me to exploit or ignore the other. These separate selves are mirrored in a world of solid atoms, literally a-tomic, indivisible and independent. The being of an atom is that it excludes all others, that all its relations are extrinsic. The new philosophy, echoing two millennia of concentrated criticism, denies that this is true. There are no literal atoms, physical or psychological. Everything that is persists in being through its relations, and could not survive in an otherwise empty universe. 'Life is communication in communion. And, conversely, isolation and lack of relationship means death for all living things, and dissolution even for elementary particles.'[22] Everything that is turns out to be informed, to have an internal structure that is related to the external manifold. My welfare is not dissociated from that of others, and there are other ways of dealing with those others than the zero-sum games (what I win, you lose) of simple games theory. 'Conserving biodiversity is definitely in our economic interests ... Our survival may depend on biodiversity. We at last recognize Whitehead's "false dichotomy: to think of nature and man".'[23] As Plato pointed out, civil association begins with a trading relationship that lets everyone profit (even if this is soon corrupted). The thesis proposed here, let me remind you, is so far from being new that it is a staple of every major philosopher since Aristotle's day. Moderns who think otherwise are as deluded as those others who think that ceremonies invented within living memory are age-old traditions.

So let us agree that entities aren't *entities*, if by that we mean only beings both independent and indivisible. Substances, as Descartes agreed, aren't *substances* in a strict sense: we are neither independent nor indivisible nor cause of our own existence. God alone is these, in Descartes's terms, and therefore alone is substance, and not a substance among many. How did he discover God? What Descartes realized was that the very fact that we can doubt our own beliefs, even our own existence, revealed a truth: namely, that there was indeed a Truth by which our thought was measured. Maybe nothing that I ordinarily suppose is true: so be it, but in that case there is still a Truth, unknown to me, by comparison with which my thought is false. My thought is imperfect, shifting, possibly self-contradictory, finite: but it is all these things because there is a perfect, unchangeable, coherent, infinite reality, *and I already know that it is so*. There could be no doubt, no error, unless there were a Real, nor could we entertain such doubt or recognize the notion of such error unless the image of the Real were stamped within our hearts. As Plato pointed out long before, I must already know what the True is if I am even to notice that my thought might not be true.[24] 'The woman who had lost a coin searched for it by the light of a lantern, but she would never have found it unless she had remembered it',[25] nor known that she had lost it. Of the Truth I only know it cannot be surpassed (as my thought can be), and cannot be denied, or thought not to exist.

Even to suggest that it might not exist (that it might not be true that there was such a thing as Truth) is indeed to talk nonsense. '*It is* and that it is impossible for it not to be, is the way of belief, for truth is its companion.'[26] As Jonathan Edwards put it, time and again:

> It seems strange sometimes to me that there should be Being from all Eternity; and I am ready to say, What need was there that any thing should be? I should then ask myself, Whether it seems strange that there should be either Something, or Nothing? If so, it is not strange that there should BE; for the necessity of there being Something, or Nothing, implies it.[27]

The presence of Being to us is revealed in our discovery that our thought stands under judgement, that our thought is often confused or self-contradictory, but yearns to repossess that which it still remembers. I have an image of Truth (and without it could not even entertain the thought that I am often wrong, that I am not the Truth): it is that eternity of which Boethius spoke, 'the whole, simultaneous and perfect possession of boundless life'.[28] Because I have that image I both can and must bring my inquiries before it, and accept such clear and distinct ideas as look most like it, always remembering that nothing in the world of my experience or yours is ever quite the Truth (for it might not be true, whereas the Truth itself is always true). 'I had promised to show you, if you recall, that there is something higher than our mind and reason. There you have it – truth itself! Embrace it if you can and enjoy it.'[29] Or as Malebranche put it: 'The truth is uncreated, immutable, immense, eternal and above all things. It is true by itself. It draws its perfection from no other thing. It renders creatures more perfect and all minds naturally seek to know it. Only God can have all these perfections. Therefore, truth is God.'[30]

The Truth, Reality, Being, God: all these terms name the one apparently undeniable, necessary something, 'the abyss of light' that Chesterton identified. 'It' is indeed Absolute: there can be nothing *else* on which it depends. But it is legitimate to wonder about its internal structure, and there are two ways of approaching the issue.[31]

The first is, so to call it, axiological. Being presents itself to us as admirable, indeed as supremely so. For those who wake, so Herakleitos said, there is one common world, but sleepers turn aside to their own private one.[32] Being of course includes our private worlds, our dreams, but absorption in such dreams at the expense of any attention to Being itself is widely recognized, even by the otherwise irreligious, as a failing. Fervent anti-realism, or fantasism, is not unknown (I have touched upon it earlier), but hardly to be recommended in the context of environmental crisis. This is not the moment to be lost in dreams. So Being, Truth, Reality is what should be attended to: if anything at all is to be valued, It must be, and must be supremely valued. The question then is: can we learn what It is by asking ourselves what we most, must admire? Being Itself must be acknowledged and admired: but if It is less admirable, less admired (as what It is) than something else, then chaos looms. To prefer anything at all to Truth is to prefer to dream. So suppose we most admire one sort, but believe that Truth is of another sort? The truth to which great scientists have testified is that Beauty is their firmest guide to truth: 'It is indeed an incredible fact that what the human mind, at its best and most profound, perceives as beautiful finds its realization in external nature.'[33] This may also serve to explain Hermann Weyl's apparently shocking claim that he had 'always tried to unite the true with the beautiful; but when [he] had to choose one or the other, [he] usually chose the beautiful'.[34] This *may* mean that he genuinely preferred to dream: I prefer to suspect that he only meant that beauty was sometimes a better guide to truth than any laborious demonstration.

If this is so (or is at least a not-unreasonable path), then we can ask what sort of thing it is we most admire. Do we in fact admire the cold and unresponsive, self-sufficient, creature? Or do we rather prefer to rank the different sorts we find according to the number and complexity of relationships that they embody? A simple pebble is united to the rest of the universe by place and gravitational influence, by reflecting light or nudging waves aside. The more we know of it the more we see relationships where none appeared before, but it will never have as many as a simple starfish, or the mammalian swimmer who picks it from the sea-floor. In the hierarchy of creation (a topic to which I shall return) it is the higher creature that is more responsive, more related to its surroundings. The ultimately valued Being, containing all things else, must be supremely responsive: not closed off, and unaffected by whatever shares in being. Describing God, Truth, Being we must incorporate this fact, that it is *more*, not less, affected by the little events around us. In waking up we increase our links with everything: the Truth to which we wake has all those links perpetually.

The second route to much the same discovery is less dependent on a doubtful assumption (that what Is must also be what's Admirable). The Truth contains all truths. To put the point in obviously (and maybe misleadingly) theistic terms: God, who is omniscient, is affected by what happens. We can of course concede that whereas our knowing something does not make it true (though it is true that if we know it then it is), 'God's knowing it' is the real cause of its being true. Any particular proposition, less theologically, is true just if it's part of the one true system of truths that identically is Reality (or perfectly reflects it). The proposition is true because Reality is thus and so: Reality is not thus because the proposition is true. But though Reality is logically prior to any proposition truly describing it, it does not remain unchanged when little facts are changed. Theologically: if God knows every truth, then He no longer knows that it is (in standard European chronometry) the Fourth of July in 1666 (because, after all, it isn't). Nor does He yet know that it is the Fourth of July in 2666 (unless perhaps by the time you read these words, it is). It seems to follow that God's knowledge is increasing all the time, and He is getting older. It is not impossible that were He confronted with a more ancient self (He must, of course, include it) He would not agree with it.

This account, a form of 'process theology', seems to some to provide a better understanding of the World and God. The 'scholastic God' is timeless and unchanging, a disconnected substance. The 'process' God is the ever-changing, infinitely connected sum of everything that happens and is done. Instead of supposing that God and the World are separate entities (after all, how could they be?), we should think of 'God' as the World-in-Unity. The world, we could say, is God's Body, or rather (since that expression intimates a theoretical gap between the body and the divine) the world is God in His corporeal being. As I live, fleetingly and ignorantly, by and in the lives of all my constituent cells and organs, so also God, though unconfusedly. Where this differs from a futile pantheism is in imputing change and improvement to that God. Things as they are are not the best they can be: God Himself is gathering Himself together from the rags of time, absorbing everything that stars and humans, wireworms, starfish and the simple pebble do. The future will never be what it once was. This, the philosophers sometimes remark, is modern Europe's (or maybe the Jewish) gift to humankind: the Greeks, they say, could not take time seriously. 'It has often rightly been emphasised that "history" was fundamentally foreign to Greek thought', so Moltmann, quite erroneously, says.[35]

It is certainly absurd to suggest that 'the Greeks' were ignorant of time's passage, or unconcerned about what happened there. But it could be argued that many philosophers, including Plato, did doubt that propositions about particulars could ever be truly known (as that the tortoiseshell cat beside me is now biting her tail). Such items were no part of divine knowledge – but not because God did not care: Plato indeed identified the notion that God did not care as a dangerous heresy. The point was rather that such particular events were not 'scientifically demonstrable': if they occurred it was not because they had to. History was the record of what actually happened, and therefore made less sense than what the poets said! We may wish to insist that the Truth does, after all, contain all truths (including ones about the tortoiseshell), and that God, in knowing them, makes them definite, but they remain, for us, beyond all argument. Even generalizations about such particulars are not ones we can prove. It does not follow that we cannot, with patience, 'know' them, but not with 'scientific knowledge'. Maybe even God cannot know them save by observation, and enactment.

'Without all doubt this world could arise from nothing but the perfectly free will of God . . . From this fountain . . . [what] we call the laws of nature have flowed, in which there appear many traces indeed of wise contrivance, but not the least shadow of necessity. These therefore we must not seek from uncertain conjectures, but learn them from observations and experiments. He who is presumptuous enough to think that he can find the true principles of physics and the laws of natural things by the force alone of his own mind, and the internal light of reason, must either suppose that the world exists by necessity, and by the same necessity follows the laws proposed; or if the order of Nature was established by the will of God, that himself, a miserable reptile, can tell what was fittest to be done.' The first thrust is levelled at the Greeks, the second at Descartes.[36]

It may be as well to remember once again that not all truth is demonstrable truth, that there are many details not to be deduced from any principle. In that sense 'the Greeks' were entirely right not to reckon history (or maybe even natural history) a 'science'. Did they err (by modern standards) in some other way?

It could perhaps be argued that till recently most thinkers did not expect great changes. As I remarked in an earlier chapter, it is apparently natural to us to believe that what we now experience is an eternal fact. Even when we realize that changes do occur, that we and all our works are mortal, we reconstruct the knowledge and are comforted.

> Cities and thrones and powers
> Stand in Time's eye,

Almost as long as flowers,
which daily die:
But as new buds put forth
To glad new men,
Out of the spent and unconsidered Earth,
The Cities rise again.

This season's Daffodil,
She never hears,
What change, what chance, what chill,
Brought down last year's:
But with bold countenance,
And knowledge small,
Esteems her seven days' continuance
To be perpetual.

So Time that is o'er-kind
To all that be,
Ordains us e'en as blind,
As bold as she:
That in our very death,
And burial sure,
Shadow to shadow, well persuaded, saith,
'See how our works endure!'[37]

Everything passes and everything returns. Even, on some accounts (the one extolled by Nietzsche, for example), the very individuals will return, doing just the same. To be at all is to be something, and every sort of finite thing has its own period, and periodicity. The notion of unending progress, fuelled by earth's capital resources and motivated by the wish for more, was not the dominant theme in any age till now. Environmentalists may wish to warn us that there are some possible discontinuities from which we won't recover, that real change is possible. But it is perhaps unwise to turn so fervently against the older picture: after all it is progress, or the ideal of progress (which is, unending change), that is giving us burning rainforests and flooded coastlands. Is not our need to rediscover limits rather than pander to the modern myth that we can go on forever without bending back upon our tracks? 'The great mistake on the part of the Marxists and of the whole of the nineteenth century lay in believing that by walking straight in front of one, one necessarily rises up into the air.'[38]

Still, we have here what looks like a real contrast. An ancient idea of perfection is circular: God alone is perfectly *causa sui*, but all lesser beings approach that perfection by repeating what they are. They reproduce themselves, or walk, like the stars, in circles, or contemplate an utterly unchanging truth. The four corners of the world are the solstices and equinoxes, and all biological life (the stars not really being biological, and yet alive) repeats itself within that cycle. The religious achieve or realize their immortality by identifying themselves entirely with the pattern of things, and so escape (if only in thought) from the grinding wheel. Absorption and escape are one and the same. From this perspective it is clear why *pleonexia* (or the dream of progress) is silly as well as self-destructive. 'More, More is the cry of a mistaken soul. Less than All will not satisfy any man.'[39] The All which we inherit through contemplative love was reckoned finite by some philosophers, but not by Plotinus. Our local and parochial worlds were fragments which yet contained the All of which they were fragments. However briefly, we could uncover Truth, and having experienced it, serve it, because the pattern of the Whole was present in each bit.

The new philosophy denies that anything is complete, even during its proper period. The point is sometimes ill-expressed, as the claim that the ancients identified things 'statically', or that they had a merely finite world. It is on the contrary a platitude that things *are* what they *do*: a knife is what can cut, a human being what can make decisions, and both exist as such most fully when they act. And whether we conceive this world as finite, like a hazelnut upon the hand of God, or infinite, without an end, is not well settled without more distinctions. But the claim is fairly clear. By one account God eternally is the sum of all perfections, and there is eternally, in Him, the perfect form of everything that He flings into time.[40] To achieve that perfection is to achieve stability and consequently, by an obvious fallacy, we think to approach perfection by preventing change. By the other account God acts and is like any other being, though universally, and His perfection lies not in stasis but in perpetual self-transcendence. Our form is not complete, and if it ever is, if its capacities for change at last run dry, that will be the end of us.[41] God, to put it crudely, may one day be bored with us, yet never – we are told – with His creative brilliance. I confess that I think but poorly of this universal and complacent parasite, pilloried by David Lindsay in *A Voyage to Arcturus*: 'The whole world of will was doomed to eternal anguish so that one being might feel joy.'[42] If God lives through and by the life of lesser beings He is subject as the rest of us to ennui or senseless rage. No doubt, as time goes on, His experience increases; by the same token His tolerance grows less.

The advantage for environmentalism of a purely immanent God is that we seem to have a clear sense in which the earth can actually be harmed. If there is a being dependent on the actual diversity of kinds then that being must be harmed by extinctions and destructions. For all we know, God's being, so understood, might be contracted or corrupted by too great a loss, as happens to Stapledon's Galactic Spirit in the war of stars and worlds.[43] If we conceive that the agonies of sentient individuals are shared and echoed by the indwelling God, and if species extinctions (even without much pain) inflict wounds on him, we give ourselves good reason to refrain. But why (advantages apart) should we believe this? We might as easily conceive that the indwelling God is taking a cure, or having his hair cut. He has precipitated or allowed vast loss before, without effect on his divinity. Nor do we know what he thinks progress. At least the God (gods?) of Abraham and the philosophers would never alter his allegiance, never change his mind. The God of process theologians always does just that, and may, for all we know, have decided to try out machines and genocide instead.

The advantages for theologians are just as doubtful. An indwelling and progressive God can be excused, perhaps, for his creation's evils. At least he shares the experience of them, and was younger when he first made the mistake. Presumably he will one day reckon his present behaviour a mistake, and look back at some now insignificant moment as a turning point. I am, I know, speaking crudely. But this conception of God, as one being, even the greatest, among many, appears to demand this crudity. There must be better ways of solving or dissolving ecological and theological crises. That God does, in some way, suffer with us, is one thing; it is another to infer that God, *qua* God, can be injured or corrupted. The whole idea makes nonsense. If there is no eternal truth or standard then God's changes, consequent upon the changes of his elements, are just that, mere changes. The doctrine is proposed to allow for real progress in the world, but instead we are bound to conclude that what seems to us corruption is as likely as 'moral development', and that there is no lasting criterion anyway by which corruption and progress are distinguishable. The suffering-with-us of such a being is no consolation.

## D The world as one and many

But still, whatever historical errors and whatever theological crudities this version of environmentalism holds, it is, I must suppose, an image of the truth. Its single great advantage is that it does appeal to people who find 'the scholastic God' absurd. The God of Abraham, as commonly conceived, was Himself not quite the schoolmen's: instead of an unresponsive and unchanging It, the Bible speaks indeed of He that Is, but as a being involved with His people's life, who urges and rebukes and may be argued with. His powers of prophecy rest on His powers to fulfil His promises, and not (or not so clearly) on His simple vision, from outside time, of what is yet to be. The God of Abraham, and of Muhammad, is also not entirely to good moderns' taste (and I shall have more to say of that hereafter). But it does provide an example, even in European tradition, of a god that seems unlike the unchanging Absolute. It has been an axiom amongst believers (even ones prepared to allegorize or question the biblical material) that God is present amongst us. Those who deny His interest in individuals or suggest that He does not care what happens to us may still retain a kind of religious feeling: the love of Being as such, without requiring that this Being return the love, is a genuine thread. Benedict Spinoza, in particular, offered an account of God and Nature (being the same thing) that some have taken as a hint for an environmentalist theology – ignoring the problem posed by Spinoza's contempt for non-human animals, and by the amoral tendencies of pantheism. Process theology purports to tread a narrow path between love of the Absolute and merely credulous worship of the Bible's God. As such, it appeals to many even without further argument.

Things as they are cannot be as they should be, despite the noble efforts of Spinoza and the Stoics to encourage that belief. But an Absolute as absolute as the scholastic God must surely have arranged things right. Better to assume that any God there is amongst us does not have absolute control. Better to assume that any God there is requires its worshippers (why else has it created or allowed them?), and can respond so swiftly to their various pleas that it is as if identical with all of them. This must appeal: we are all God, or part of God, and all of us contribute to the total glory, to the work that we are doing everywhere. We can even entertain the thought that there is, as yet, no unity beyond the barest co-presence of everything across the world. Does any information pass faster than the speed of light, even God's? Perhaps the different elements of God have not been together since the very beginning, and now live in hope of recapturing community through interstellar traffic. A God like that is apparently easier to believe in than a truly 'supernatural' one (not limited by any natural laws), especially since that aspect of divinity with which we deal is only our higher self, not linked (as yet) with any stranger god-mind. The Single God (who will still be a union of all the holy ones – as the Tibetan lamas told their visitor[44]) is now a hope, and not a given fact. That God, we may hope, will remember us, and care for us, with rather more attention than we give our own constituent cells – though I am puzzled as to why it should give *us* more attention than it gives those cells.

Hartshorne himself, in whom process theology had its beginning, would add that we must after all conceive that there is an eternal aspect to God, if only to avoid the problem I identified (that if everything changes, including what Beauty is, then there can be no progress).[45] But that concession throws us back to the scholastic God, who was both immanent and transcendent, incorruptible but always responsive. If the scholastic God is incoherent so is Hartshorne's own. I doubt, in any case, if those who adopt the process God as theirs are really endorsing Hartshorne rather than laying claim to a popular theology that matches their desire to praise a plural God. The poet Yeats identified this age of the world as one where divinity would be seen as multiform, inchoate, uncertain where to go. Whatever its abstract failings, maybe this creed will serve environmental ends? The New Thing will be born from all that the former age rejected, 'from all that [his] stories symbolize as a harlot, and would take after its mother; because we had worshipped a single god it would worship many or receive from Joachim de Flora's Holy Spirit a multitudinous influx'.[46]

The plural quality of God, and the fact that 'it' acts and is only through existing beings and to no predetermined end, all add up to a doctrine that perhaps supports environmentalism. The older humanistic theism, whatever qualms it may have felt about our worth, found God at work in human, personal encounter, and dreamed of a day when God would be in the midst of us (us human beings, that is). But a God that works through all its elements to no predetermined end will remember the blackbird or the tortoiseshell as well as us. All of us are fellow-travellers in what Leopold called 'the odyssey of evolution'.[47] In this the creed is biblical. In the Book of Job 'Yahweh described himself as the wisdom that makes for the survival of the wild ass, the hamster, the eagle, the ostrich, of all living nature, and the wisdom that uproots mountains and annihilates angels'.[48] The vision of things before which Job bows his head is of a cosmic democracy, in which each creature gets its due and is allowed its own integrity. There is still too much of overmastering power here to please the process theologian, but the power is shown within creation, not on top. To recognize God there, amongst the least of these His little ones, amounts to accepting their reality, their presence with us upon equal terms. This last and greatest 'liberation movement' restores conviviality (in principle, if not in dreadful fact).[49]

More is meant by this than moderns usually admit, however. Much of the doctrine can be allegorized in terms that any materialist scientist can, at a pinch, accept. On the one hand, there is an absolute equality amongst bits of matter: there is nothing special about the stuff that makes 'us' up. All of us are star-stuff, our elements manufactured in stars that exploded long before the earth was formed. On the other, we may (if we wish) declare that 'the grand design of nature perceived broadly in four dimensions to include the forces that move the universe and created man, with special focus on evolution in our own biosphere is something intrinsically good that it is right to preserve and enhance, and wrong to destroy'.[50] But process theology, if it is to have a real basis, requires something more than material equality and a declaration of loyalty to unnamed and unexamined forces. Particularly it requires an account of consciousness.

This is the major sticking point for modernists. Descartes noticed his own existence as a thinking thing, as Augustine and many others had before.[51] He guessed, and Malebranche believed, that non-human animals were not thus thinking things. Those not in the grip of theory have usually thought this absurd. Dogs may not think about theorems, but they have their thoughts, their feelings: there is 'something it is like to be a dog', there is someone (as it were) 'at home'. The problem for philosophy of mind is to identify the regular relationship between the world of 'matter in motion' and the realm of thought. Those for whom the process-God is only a way of speaking need not worry (much): to say that God is working His purpose out in all the myriad centres of existence is only to express a moral solidarity with what we see of it. 'God' only names our projected spirit, our sympathy. Even to say that pigs can suffer pain is only, on this account, to choose to include them among the things we bother about. 'To attribute feelings to X is only to remind ourselves that it is wrong to hurt X [which is to say, respectable people don't usually approve of doing it].'[52] The alternative is to insist that it requires a selective blindness of the soul to say that 'animals' (who are our biological kin) don't think or feel, and maybe that the god-blind have a similar disease. Seeing the world as god-filled is like seeing one's human or non-human friend as sentient: it requires a movement of the heart as well as of the head.

But the issue here is *how* a material world can generate consciousness. The material world, after all, is posited (since Descartes) as a realm of matter in motion, having such properties as do not depend on any sentient's sensing. Having posited that world (which we can never experience like that) we are naïvely startled to discover that none of the properties left to it are linked, by any necessary connection, to the properties we sense or the fact of sensing them. If we can understand what it is for a thing to be (say) square, in motion, weighing so and so much, without having any reason to impute to it a colour, an aesthetic value or a real identity, then we can hardly be surprised that those latter things don't follow from, and aren't explained by any properties we have imputed. So any connection there is between the merely material properties and the experienced ones must be brute fact, not something to be anticipated by the use of reason. But such brute facts can only be learned from experience. Even if we are content to admit brute facts in our ontology (and thereby admit magic) what reason have we to believe there is any such conjunction? We never actually experience the merely material: if it does not explain experience why posit it?

It follows that it is not Cartesian *mind* that is absurd, but Cartesian matter. The only physical being that it is sensible to posit is a being that requires its being experienced. Matter could never exist without mind, though many of the minds (much of the mind) associated with inorganic matter (if it exists at all) must, I suppose, be very unlike ours. It seems to follow, then, that we have after all good reason to think that there is an 'inner life' in every thing. Process theology is, in effect, panpsychist. There has never been a world without its 'inner', never a merely material set of properties. Whether that 'inner' allows for real unity across the universe, or 'the universe' is itself only a pious hope (as not yet being unitary), who knows? Bodies are not things weirdly attached to minds: 'Man has no body distinct from his soul; for that call'd body is a portion of soul discern'd by the five senses, the chief inlets of soul in this age.'[53] Which is also, incidentally, Plato's view. To see anything, any thing at all, is to see a sister:

> Each grain of Sand,
> Every Stone on the Land,
> Each rock & each hill,
> Each fountain & rill,
> Each herb & each tree,
> Mountain, hill, earth & sea,
> Cloud, Meteor & Star,
> Are Men seen Afar.[54]

And on the other hand,

> . . . the Jewels of Light,
> Heavenly Men beaming bright,
> Appear'd as One Man
> Who complacent began
> My limbs to enfold
> In his beams of bright gold.[55]

That One Man, in Blake's more orthodox moments, is Jesus, the Divine Imagination in whom 'all things are comprehended in their Eternal Forms'.

It is possible, in brief, to construct some reasons (political and philosophical) for believing a sort of process theology. In its least orthodox form, it is a sort of panpsychism, which holds out the hope (but only that) of an eventual unity. To avoid reducing history to a drunkard's walk to no clear end we must perhaps insist, as Plato did, that there are eternal values even if everything particular changes. Without that changelessness, and without any realistic hope of any eventual community, we must be like those fabled travellers who set sail toward a beacon that cannot be reached because it does not really exist.[56] To travel hopefully cannot be better than to arrive: what then could we hope for? In making that change we move 'process theology' back toward a more orthodox theology, complete with whatever flaws that doctrine had.

But my worry remains. The advantage of the process-god is that so many moderns find it easy to accept. But that is partly because it feeds on *pleonexia*, and on the myth of progress. 'New age' thinkers may sometimes pay lip-service to the 'value' of material being, but their creed lends more support to the dreams of 'hominization'. Chardin, in particular, is not any sort of environmentalist, dark or light green. He was, in effect, an industrialist, and one that looked to collectivist solutions for our salvation. Once again, the proposed cure is perhaps itself a symptom. *Pleonexia* is probably what Greens often mean by 'industrialism', which bears the same relation to industry as scientism to science. This invites ridicule, since we can all see that it is industry, and especially capitalist industry, that has done more for us all than any socio-political system on record – though it also impoverishes multitudes.

> If there is one notion that virtually every successful politician on earth – socialist or fascist or capitalist – agrees on, it is that 'economic growth' is good, necessary, the proper end of organised human activity. But where does economic growth end? It ends at – or at least it runs straight through – the genetically engineered dead world that the optimists envision.[57]

It is that death of nature that we should fear, and therefore suspect what leads to it – even if it comes clothed in sympathetic, hopeful and panpsychist form.

## Notes

1. See my *The Nature of the Beast* (Oxford University Press: Oxford, 1980).

2. I. Bradley, *God Is Green* (Darton, Longman & Todd: London, 1990), p. 36.

3. S. McDonagh, *The Greening of the Church* (Geoffrey Chapman: London, 1990), p. 48.

4. M. Fox, *Creation Spirituality* (Harper: San Francisco, 1991) p. 102.

5. R. Descartes, *Philosophical Letters*, ed. A. Kenny (Clarendon Press: Oxford, 1970), p. 128: January 1642.

6. R. Descartes, Letter to Elizabeth, dated 28 June 1643; cited by M. Grene, *Descartes* (Harvester: Brighton, 1985), p. 19.

7. John G. Neihart (ed.) *Black Elk Speaks* (Abacus: London, 1974; first published 1932; copyright University of Nebraska, 1961).

8. *Black Elk*, p. 16.

9. B. McKibben, *The End of Nature* (Penguin: Harmondsworth, 1990), p. 159.

10. Plato, *Laws* 903cd; see Aristotle, *Nicomachean Ethics* 6.1141a20ff.

11. G. M. Hopkins, 'Pied Beauty' in W. H. Gardner and N. H. Mackenzie (eds), *Poems of Gerard Manley Hopkins* (Oxford University Press: London, 1970; fourth edition), pp. 69–70.

12. R. Harré, *Personal Being* (Harvard University Press: Boston, 1984), p. 88.

13. W. Berry, *What Are People For?* (Rider Books: London, 1990), p. 113.

14. Plato, *Laws* 5.740; see also 6.761. Diogenes Laertius, *Lives of the Philosophers* 3.15f. testifies that Plato believed that 'living creatures could

not have survived unless they had apprehended the idea, and had been endowed by nature with intelligence to that end': wisdom is not confined to humankind.

15. Plato, *Politicus* 263c.

16. Fox, *Creation Spirituality*, p. 17.

17. Plotinus, *Enneads*, tr. S. Mackenna (Faber: London, 1956), VI.7.22, 24–31.

18. See G. Sircello, *A New Theory of Beauty* (Princeton University Press: Princeton and London, 1975), pp. 81ff.

19. Plotinus, *Enneads* I.6.4. 1956 edn, p. 59.

20. See V. Eller, *Christian Anarchy* (Eerdmans: Grand Rapids, MI, 1987).

21. W. Wink, *Naming the Powers* (Philadelphia: Fortress Press, 1984), p. 115.

22. J. Moltmann, *God in Creation*, tr. M. Kohl (SCM: London, 1985), p. 3.

23. C. Patten (1990); quoted by J. Phillipson, 'The natural world', p. 197, in B. Cartledge (ed.), *Monitoring the Environment* (Oxford University Press: Oxford, 1992), pp. 193–206.

24. Plato, *Meno* 80eff.

25. Augustine, *Confessions* 10.18, tr. R. S. Pine-Coffin (Harmondsworth: Penguin, 1961), p. 224.

26. Parmenides, as quoted by K. Raine, *The Inner Journey of the Poet* (Allen & Unwin: London, 1982), p. 104, after Gerard Manley Hopkins.

27. J. Edwards, *Basic Writings*, ed. O. E. Winslow (New American Library: New York, 1966), p. 51; see also pp. 45f: 'if any man thinks he Can think well Enough how there should be nothing I'll Engage that what he means by nothing is as much something as any thing that ever He thought of in his Life.'

28. Boethius, *Tractates and Consolation of Philosophy*, tr. H. F. Stewart, E. K. Rand and S. J. Tester (London: Heinemann Loeb Classical Library, 1973), 5.6.9.

29. Augustine, *De Libero Arbitrio* 2.13.35 in *The Teacher, The Free Choice of the Will and Grace and Free Will* (Washington: Catholic University of America Press, 1968), p. 144.

30. N. Malebranche, *The Search after Truth*, tr. T. M. Lennon and P. J. Olscamp (Ohio State University: Columbus, 1980), p. 234 (3.2.6).

31. See C. Hartshorne, *The Divine Relativity* (Yale University Press: New Haven, 1948).

32. Herakleitos 22B89 DK: see my *God's World and the Great Awakening* (Clarendon Press: Oxford, 1991), pp. 51f.

33. S. Chandrasekhar, *Truth and Beauty* (University of Chicago Press: Chicago, 1987), p. 66.

34. Chandrasekhar, ibid., p. 52, quoting Freeman Dyson's quotation of Weyl. Compare Dostoyevsky's preference for Christ over the true, or the provably true, in *Letters to Family and Friends* (Chatto & Windus: London, 1962), p. 71.

35. J. Moltmann, *Theology of Hope*, tr. J. W. Leitch (SCM Press: London, 1967), p. 259.

36. Newton represented by Hooykaas, after Cotes's preface to second edition of *Principia*: R. Hooykaas, *Religion and the Rise of Modern Science* (Scottish Academic Press: Edinburgh, 1972), p. 49.

37. R. Kipling, 'Cities and Thrones and Powers' in *Verse: 1885–1926* (Hodder & Stoughton: London, 1927), p. 479.

38. S. Weil, *Notebooks*, tr. A. Wills (Routledge & Kegan Paul; London, 1956), vol. II, p. 447.

39. W. Blake, *Writing*, p. 97.

40. I must emphasize that 'God' here names the God of the Philosophers, pagan as well as Abrahamic: some would say that God is *not* the God of Abraham. If they exist they are of course identical, but it may be true that, as ideas, they are not.

41. See J. B. McDaniel, *Of God and Pelicans* (Westminster/John Knox Press: Louisville, 1989), p. 46.

42. D. Lindsay, *A Voyage to Arcturus* (Pan: London, 1974; 1st edn 1963), p. 286.

43. O. Stapledon, *Starmaker* (Methuen: London, 1937).

44. I. Kant, *Political Writings*, ed. H. Reiss (Cambridge University Press: Cambridge, 1970), p. 107, quoting Francisco Orazio.

45. See (for a far more sympathetic treatment than mine) D. A. Dombrowski, *Hartshorne and the Metaphysics of Animal Rights* (State University of New York: Albany, 1988).

46. W. B. Yeats, *Explorations* (Macmillan: London, 1962), p. 393; see my *Civil Peace and Sacred Order* (Clarendon Press: Oxford, 1989), p. 31.

47. A. Leopold, *Sand County Almanac* (Oxford University Press: New York, 1968), p. 109.

48. H. M. Kallen, 'The Book of Job' in N. N. Glatzer, *The Dimensions of Job* (Schocken Books: New York, 1969), pp. 17ff. See *Civil Peace*, p. 147.

49. See Charles Birch and John B. Cobb, *The Liberation of Life* (Cambridge University Press; Cambridge, 1981).

50. R. Sperry, *Science and Moral Priority* (Blackwell: Oxford, 1982), p. 22.

51. See 'Descartes' debt to Augustine' in M. McGhee (ed.), *Philosophy, Religion and the Spiritual Life* (Cambridge University Press: Cambridge, 1992), pp. 73–88.

52. D. A. Dombrowski, *The Philosophy of Vegetarianism* (University of Massachusetts Press: Amherst, 1984), p. 129, summarizing R. Rorty, *Philosophy and the Mirror of Nature* (Princeton University Press: Princeton, 1979), pp. 182–92. Words within square brackets are my own summary of what conventionalism must mean.

53. W. Blake, 'Marriage of Heaven and Hell' §4 in *Complete Writings*, ed. G. Keynes (Clarendon Press: Oxford, 1966), p. 149.

54. Blake, Letter to Butts (2 October 1800), ibid., pp. 804f.

55. Blake, 'Vision of the Last Judgement', ibid., pp. 605f.

56. N. O. Lossky, *The World As an Organic Whole* (Oxford University Press: London, 1928), p. 198.

57. McKibben, *End of Nature*, p. 159.

# The crown of creation

............................5

............................

## A The charms of Mega-Big

In seeking to set out the force, and the failures, of an environmentalist theology that draws on process philosophy, I neglected to address
one central thème. What is the point of creation? I spoke rather
vaguely (in the spirit of that creed) of 'God's gathering himself
together', of an eventual 'unity', and it may be admitted that these
images do speak to us, and that (perhaps) they encourage a kinder,
gentler world. Has any more orthodox theology a better story? How
could it have?

If 'God' is the name of Being, Truth, Reality, we have some chance
of proving that 'He' is: at any rate, the claim that He isn't makes no
sense. The use of a personal pronoun may be dangerous (as more
than born-again atheists have said): Weil points out that 'if the "I", in
the personal sense, fades away in proportion and in so far as man
imitates God, how could it be sufficient to conceive of a personal
God? The image of a personal God is a hindrance to such imitation.'[1]
Impersonally conceived, how can God have any purposes at all?
'Creation' might as well be 'emanation': from the bare fact of being,
the abyss of light, stem all the little facts and figments, but not
to satisfy an insufficiency in God. Even if we allow a little more
'personhood' in Being Itself (even if, as I argued in my previous

chapter, we have to admit that consciousness is as fundamental as anything else and does not need to wait in the wings till 'mere matter' can produce it), how can Being-Mind-Joy (the ancient Hindu name for It) be insufficient by itself? In scholastic thought, and similarly, God cannot be improved by any addition since He is already, and from eternity, that Being than which none greater can be conceived. A being that can be improved cannot, in scholastic eyes, be God. Creation can only be the unfolding or publication of goods He already has. Nor can there be any reason to require a creation that develops, that is 'better' now than then. If the world's origin is outside time, and perfect, then earlier stages can be just as good, if any of them are good, as later ones. There is even an easy confusion possible, to suppose that earlier stages, being closer to the origin, are better than what comes by decay and falling-off much later on. It is a confusion because what comes earlier in the temporal order is, by this account, no closer to the eternal origin. And that origin is only mythically represented as a 'time before' the fall, the Norman conquest, the enclosures or the Second World War. If Being-Mind-Joy transcends time then every moment of time arises from eternity, and owes nothing to any previous moment. Our impression that things now are caused by things a moment earlier is as erroneous as the belief (if anyone has it) that one frame of a moving picture is caused by another. The frames may tell a consistent story, but that is by the narrator's choice. God's reason, if He needs reasons, for creating such a world as this can neither be to add goods to His glory, nor *a fortiori* to add goods by development that He could not add by fiat.

The repeated claim of liberal theologians[2] who attempt theodicy that even God could not create His saints by fiat, but must instead rely on the painful growth and self-correction of evolutionary ages and historical time, assumes a God quite unlike the tradition's, but one that might provide a better answer to the problem, why God would create. The only way for us, or for an anthropomorphic deity, to create moral intelligences, might well be to initiate an evolutionary process whereby trial and error might mysteriously bring the thing about. Certainly the most convincing fiction about 'machine intelligence' imagines such a process: witness Poul Anderson's 'Epilogue', where self-replicating machines, in a world purged of organic life, eventually reproduce, with their distinctive nuance, a replica of this our present biosphere, including moral intelligence.[3] If the modern story of our descent is intelligible, so is that – but we are of course no closer than before to conceiving how it happens. Maybe other fantasies are true, and the whole temporal biosphere, including us, was indeed devised by a world engineer who doesn't know how things work, but only that, with sufficient time, they often do. Maybe that engineer has purposes of its own: perhaps to produce food, or bait for still more sinister beings, or what you will. Maybe it farms us as we farm other beings. But such a being, even if we had reason to believe in it, could not stand in for God. As yet another finite, ignorant being of unknown purposes it cannot be that being than which none greater, worthier can be conceived. If there is a god like that (Super-Yeti or Mega-Big, Galactic Engineers) then we can perhaps forgive it, but should not take its methods or mentality as any guide to life. Perhaps there is no escape for us from Mega-Big, but then we must despair indeed. Not knowing even what it wants or what its powers are, we cannot practically defy it, but we must wish we could (as we cannot even wish, once we have thought it through, to 'defy th'Omnipotent to arms'). In that extremity the Hebrews called on God, the God of Justice, and Gautama Buddha looked beyond the gods to the Unborn, and Indestructible. Chesterton's Alfred, incognito in the camp of the invading Danes:

> Riseth up against realm and rod,
> A thing forgotten, a thing downtrod,
> The last, lost giant, even God,
> Is risen against the world.

The two roots of traditional Abrahamic theism are here agreed. Being Itself cannot be identified with an ignorant world-engineer. Yahweh cannot be on the side of the oppressor. The time-bound engineering deity is better called the Devil.

What seemed at first to be theodicy, a justifying of the ways of God, ends by exalting naked power directed, without moral limits, to an unknown end. We, being discontented with our present state but not knowing what is missing or able to discover it in ourselves, might initiate a cosmic experiment, typified by pain, predation and decay, to see if something better might emerge. We might even dip into the lives we ruined, like connoisseurs of horror films, and pack them away like Stapledon's Starmaker, half-satisfied and half-dissatisfied with the inelegance of their solutions. Stapledon's star-travelling sages, united in the cosmic spirit at the end of time, beheld this horror, the goal and sink of all heroic endeavour, 'and yet [they] worshipped'. I find this impossible.

## B The evolutionary argument

But maybe I am being unfair. I have emphasized that we do not know our maker's purposes (if there are any), nor how he achieved them. Process theologians may reasonably reply that this, by some accounts of knowledge, must be so. Our grasp of the maker's purpose rests not on any prior understanding of 'his' nature, but on historical evidence and personal faith. A criticism that applies to every creed (including the most materialistic) is no good reason to disbelieve this one. So what is the evidence? As far as I can see it is threefold: the evolutionary record, personal life, and the metaphysics that I sketched before.

Environmentalism, a delight and care for all the living world, predates evolutionary theory. But the particular shape that it most often takes today is deeply informed by popular biological thought. The realization of our place in terrestrial (and celestial) history accompanies a realization of our place in the contemporary biosphere: 'at the top' or 'in the centre', maybe, but definitely 'within'. We are part, as Chief Seattle did not say, of the web of life. How is it woven?

Terrestrial and celestial history can be conceived as the increase of complexity. Quarks unite in hadrons and leptons; they in atoms; atoms in molecules; molecules in yet more complex molecules like those of DNA; these in prokaryotic and then in eukaryotic cells; and so to multi-cellular organisms, swarms, hives and political societies. Alongside the increase in complexity (that is, of heterogenous parts within and manifold information tracks without), we are told, there is an increase in intensity and richness of experience. The most advanced example of this linear process known to us are human beings themselves, ourselves, in personal communion. The universe is busily creating people. The process is unilinear and progressive, and if the original condition of things had been even a little different (as it might, mathematically, have been) no such process would have happened. There therefore seems good reason to suppose that the universe was meant to make us, and who but a being as least as 'complex' could consider this? In so far as we desire to maintain our being (and that is what every entity does) we must maintain the process, care for the whole that makes us and which we were made to care for.

I almost wish that I could believe this story. I certainly prefer it to that other answer to the 'anthropic puzzle' (that the universe seems to have been 'fine-tuned' to allow our genesis), which is to postulate the real existence of all possible originals and all possible laws. In such a world it would be no surprise that the fragment we inhabited was suitable for us – although the bare fact of being would be as inscrutable. The people who do believe it may show greater concern for 'nature' than do those who believe (or act as if they believed) that we are only tourists, owing nothing to the land we tread upon. But there are at least three obstacles to belief.

First that human life has so far occupied such an infinitesimally small part of available time and space as to make it doubtful that *we* could be the point of things. For all we know our life is an anomaly, a byproduct or quaint irrelevance. We might as well say, with the Cargo Culters of the Pacific Islands, that twentieth-century technology was a gift of the gods to them, stolen in transit by the Europeans.

> If you lived in the garden of Eden, or even in, say Fort Lauderdale, you might be able to think that the earth had been made for you and your pleasure. But not if you lived in the desert of the southwest. If the desert was made for you, why is there so little water? It's infinitely more likely that the desert was made for buzzards.[4]

And the sky for stars.

Second, the story rests on incoherent postulates. On the one hand, it takes a universe of unimaginable age and size to produce such complex beings as ourselves; on the other the universe was, from the first, designed by a being more complex than ourselves. Either complexity is not a precondition of creative agency, or else it is. If it is not (as all *traditional* theists think), a creator-god can plan the future from His absolute simplicity, but does not need a universe to make His images. If it is, then a universe may be necessary, but there can be no creator till long after the creation.[5] Fantasists occasionally explore the notion that the World-Spirit formed through evolutionary ages may transcend time, and at last begin the process that produced It. But this is actually to name the world itself as *causa sui*, and is really only a mythological version of assorted 'bootstrap' theories invented by physicists desperate to avoid the eternal God. It may help us to think like this, but the notion eliminates the advantage for theodicy of process thought. If the God that made the world 'in the beginning' is after all the final version that will emerge at the end, then it has all the faults of both the process-god and the scholastic one. On the one hand it knows what follows the creation, and on the other it is subject to natural constraints not of its making. It is neither Being nor a forgivably ignorant being. It can be forgiven only if it, literally, has to do these things: but then, we have to do things too, and can forgive ourselves the crisis we have brought. All these pictures tend to turn into the Stoic creed: that God-and-Nature is exactly and determinedly what is, and that it passes through a phase when everything is united (technically, the conflagration) and a much longer one when the unity seems to be lost. A slight modification of the Stoic picture (in which there is a finite span of time, looped round upon itself) can give us an infinite (?) stretch of aeons, each marginally different from the others, and only some of them inhabited (the 'many aeons' hypothesis, to go with the 'many worlds'). There is of course no evidence at all for any of this, nor reason to believe it except the need not to believe in God.

The third objection is that, after all, there is good reason to doubt that evolutionary history is unilinear and progressive. It turns out to be marked by catastrophe and unpredictable change. One of Steven Jay Gould's most recent books, *Wonderful Life*,[6] is a study of the rediscovery and re-interpretation of the fossils of the Burgess Shale of British Columbia, first discovered and then wholly misrepresented by C. D. Walcott in 1909. Walcott believed that those fossils were of primitive life-forms easily assignable to modern phyla, and sustained this preconception by making himself believe that missing parts had been destroyed, or that separate organisms were expectable appendages. Only in the 1970s, when Harry Whittington and his research students began to re-examine the fossil evidence, did it gradually emerge that many of the Burgess Shale organisms represented radically unfamiliar genera, orders, phyla that seemed to be as complex and hard-wearing as those that could plausibly be assigned to modern, surviving phyla. Gould concludes from his study that we are not necessary to the world, and should adopt a different attitude to ourselves than, he says, tradition offers us. If the Cambrian creatures had evolved even a little differently there would be no human beings at all, nor anything much like them. The world would be as full without us. We are not what 'evolution' aimed at, nor were our ancestors better suited to survive than all their unknown cousins. We have survived a primordial shipwreck, but by no virtue of ours, or theirs.

The usual response to this, as Gould knows, is to say that Darwinian selection 'guarantees' that those who survive were 'fitter' than the rest. It doesn't. No doubt there is Darwinian selection. But there are also catastrophes, both local and global, in which those who survive need have no distinctive, genetically determined traits in common, or none that give them any normal advantage over those that perished. Living things diversify and are cut down, only to diversify again from within the narrower confines of the surviving body-plans. What we had viewed as 'the growing tip of evolution' turns out to be a surviving twig, 'the last gasp of a richer ancestry'.[7] We have no good reason to believe that past ecosystems or past organisms were less 'complex' than the present. On the contrary, as far back as we can actually see, the world of life, the world itself, was already complex beyond imagination. The gardener has not always selected her preferred twigs, nor imposed a selective pressure that reliably picks out only those twigs with a certain distinctive property. Sometimes she has just chopped away, and the survivors can boast no special reason for their escape even if, by chance, they do turn out to have distinctive features. The thought is not a new one. Even Stapledon, who played ingenious games with optimistic evolutionary theory to suggest that human intelligence would always re-evolve, included in his fantasies occasions when the future of the species was determined by sheer chance. Thus, some hundred thousand years in the future the Patagonian civilization, and the first human species, are brought to an abrupt end by a nuclear accident. 'Of the two hundred million members of the human race all were burnt or roasted or suffocated within three months – all but thirty-five, who happened to be in the neighbourhood of the North Pole.'[8] From those thirty-five, after ten million years, sprang – or would spring – the second human species. If it had chanced to be a different thirty-five, or not on the coast of Labrador, things would have been entirely different, but it would be merely superstitious to imagine that there must be a reason, in the constitution of those thirty-five, why they survived and not two hundred million others.[9]

Even those Darwinians who place less weight on catastrophe as the engine of evolutionary change agree with Gould that evolution was probably not orthogenetic. There is no single measurement by which we could say that later organisms are uniformly 'better' or 'fitter' than earlier forms. The widely diffused notion that complexity or sociality or sheer intelligence increases over time is probably ideological in origin. There may be periods when it does, or does in particular lineages, as there have been times and lineages when size increased. Maybe we can track the ancestors of horses by their smooth passage from five-toed quadrupeds to creatures running on the tips of their single surviving digits. But need we suppose that their descendants would remain like that, or take to skates? Perhaps they will have grown new toes, and taken to climbing trees? Maybe there will one day be sea-horses with hoofs tucked well inside, like whales. Maybe our descendants, so far from being more intelligent, will have been selected for some presently invisible difference, or differences. It is all too easy to believe that we, being human, are the central thread of evolutionary history, that we are the 'most evolved' of creatures, and that other things are 'more primitive' the less they resemble us. But the truth is that every contemporary organism has an evolutionary past as long, as convoluted and as unpredictable as we. There are no primitive life-forms, and we are not 'more evolved' than anyone else. Even creatures who, as far as we can tell, are a lot more like their remoter ancestors than we are like ours, have had an evolutionary history. Since we know practically nothing about their ancestors' actual behaviour, we do not know whether the resemblance is more than structural. Oddly enough, when it suits us we still lay claim to having an early, unspecialized form: that is, we claim to be the unchanged originals. When the opposite opinion suits us, we pretend to be the 'growing tip of evolution', time's latest offspring. All such ideas are echoes at once of fairy-tales, and of Aristotelian common-sense: that human beings display the basic form of life most clearly, that every other earthly creature is a failed attempt at human life (very much as women are maimed males!), that it is in human life that the point of the universe is unveiled. I shall return to that strange doctrine, but I certainly don't want to reaffirm it in the usual form.

To make his point Gould imagines several alternative histories.[10] Instead of annelids, the priapulids (which were the world's first soft-bodied carnivores) might have triumphed. Instead of the mammalian carnivores who succeeded the mysteriously extinguished dinosaurs, there might have been (as once there were, in South America) carnivorous diatrymids. 'We can invent stories about two legs, bird brains and no teeth as necessarily inferior to all fours and sharp canines, but we know in our heart of hearts that if birds had won, we could tell just as good a tale about their inevitable success.'[11]

Even on more orthodox Darwinian theory, leaving the randomly selective effect of cataclysm aside, there is no need for useful variations to occur just when they did. Prokaryotic cells dominated the fossil record for two billion years, before the complex co-operative endeavour of the eukaryotic cell, and later still the multicellular organisms began. It might, for all we can tell, have happened sooner or later; if it had taken much longer then the sun might have ended its biologically useful life before there were metazoans remotely like ourselves.[12] Maybe it actually happened again and again, but the new-born eukaryote or metazoan perished, by chance, before it had produced a large enough population to be genuinely subject to non-random, statistical selection.

The Drunkard's Walk of evolutionary change need not have ended here, or anywhere much like here. 'In an entirely literal sense, we owe our existence, as large and reasoning mammals, to our lucky stars.'[13] Even when there were hominids, there need not have been ourselves;

> Run the tape again, and let the tiny twig of *Homo sapiens* expire in Africa. Other hominids may have stood on the threshold of what we know as human possibilities, but many sensible scenarios would never generate our level of mentality. Run the tape again, and this time Neanderthal perishes in Europe and *Homo erectus* in Asia (as they did in our world). The sole surviving stock, *Homo erectus* in Africa, stumbles along for a while, even prospers, but does not speciate and therefore remains stable. A mutated virus then wipes *Homo erectus* out, or a change in climate reconverts Africa into inhospitable forest. One little twig on the mammalian branch, a lineage with interesting possibilities that were never realized, joins the vast majority of species in extinction. So what? Most possibilities are never realized, and who will ever know the difference?[14]

We might never have existed; we might not exist for long. We are, as tradition taught us, utterly contingent. Not only we as individuals, but we as a species and as a natural kind (the kind of Rational Being) may perish utterly, and 'who would tell the difference?'. 'Some find the prospect depressing. I [he says] have always regarded it as exhilarating, and a source of both freedom and consequent moral responsibility.'[15] I do not quite see why, or how, or what is meant by 'freedom and responsibility' in a world like that. I think – rather uncertainly – that Gould's reasoning is as follows. If we were the product of a plan, if anyone or anything had intended us to be, then, on the one hand, our designer was both cruel and astoundingly circuitous, and on the other, there would be a way of being which was ineluctably intended for us. We would be someone else's plan, and compelled to think our planner was monstrous.

The conclusion seems to be that we have at least less evidence than process-thinkers think to suppose that we, or anything much like us, is 'the point' of evolution. If Gould is right we even have some reason to *hope* that we are not. It is earth's contingency that wakens love: the sense that what we love might not have been at all, and is now mortal. A comment of Weil's is relevant (and also to the kind of nationalism that I described in an earlier chapter): 'One can either love France for the glory which would seem to ensure for her a prolonged existence in time and space; or else one can love her as something which, being earthly, can be destroyed, and is all the more precious on that account.'[16] Rather than identify ourselves, grandiloquently, with an unchallengeable movement toward the future, better have smaller, quieter loves. Rather than seeking a religious form which gives us reason to think that we can't do much harm, better believe we can. The scholastic God is in no need of us, and neither is the universe. There is no planned denouement – though there may be a moment when the world is changed.

## C The form of personal being

A moment ago I used the phrase 'the natural kind that is Rational Being'. For there is a possible response to Gould that links up with the second argument for the religious ideology I am describing. Biological species are not themselves natural kinds: they are simply sets of interbreeding populations largely isolated from the wider gene-pool in which, not so long before, they swam. Conspecific animals do not necessarily have any single property in common, except that they are members of the same set of populations. Unless we believe that species were created separately, we must conclude that they have shared ancestors: I am – obviously – conspecific with my remotest hominid ancestors, and they with the ancestors of chimpanzees and gorillas. Being 'of a different species' is an accident: if other hominid clusters had survived we would be in no doubt that the 'higher primates' were (technically) a ring-species, with fertile and infertile crosses.[17] The genetic isolation of particular groups enables them to grow differently over time, though they are never (it turns out) as isolated as we once thought. Genetic material crosses species-boundaries by viral infection, not miscegenation.

So species are not natural kinds (not even the human species). But it does not follow that there are none. Marsupial wolves are enough like wolves to pass, and I see no special reason to insist that human beings (or humanoid, if you prefer) could not have been *feathered* bipeds (descended from the diatrymids)! 'Hydrocarbon arachnoids from Jupiter are men [by which I meant humans] as well as we, if they can converse with us and we with them', as I remarked in summary of Aristotle.[18] There may be natural kinds, in other words, which lineages variously instantiate, by which they are guided. Think of it like this: there may be many ways to make a radio receiver, but what tune it plays is not dictated solely by its constitution. Radios that can play no tune at all are junked; what tune they play is limited by the range to which they are tuned; and the same tunes will be heard from many different radios. Our genes may still contain the possibility of generating rabbits, sea-squirts and bats (or rather neo-rabbits, quasi-squirts and werbats): the tune they are currently playing is the old favourite called Humanity.

Gould suggests that there are possible worlds where beings like us did not evolve, because (for example) *Pikaia*, the first recorded chordate and our putative ancestor, perished without issue.[19] In that case our particular species (being defined by its actual ancestry) would certainly not be here, but does it really follow that there would have been no land-based, upright, tool-using, social and parentally affectionate, verbalizing, curious creatures indistinguishably like ourselves? If my parents had not met, or had not had a third male child, I would not be here (and, obviously, not be missed), but would there be no one at all sufficiently like me? If *Pikaia*'s survival did not guarantee our being (because there were many unpredictable chances between then and now), *Pikaia*'s extinction certainly cannot guarantee the non-being of beings just like us. If we cannot tell from looking at *Aysheaia* (another arthropod of the Burgess Shale) that there would one day be things like butterflies, bees and beetles, how can we tell by looking at *Marella, Leanchoilia* and *Sidneyia* (creatures without known, actual descendants) that there won't?[20]

But why believe that Rationality or Humanity names such a repeatable kind? Distinct sorts of (popularly called) fish (namely *agnatha, chondrichthyes, osteichthyes*), ichthyosaurs, whales, dolphins, seals all approximate, from different ancestries, to one general kind, continually resummoned from the happy nothing. Are people a similar evocation? If they are, how often have they happened in earth's past, or up amongst the star-folk? We have no evidence of either. So maybe we are a fluke, not something that is to be expected anywhere (as fish-things are, wherever there is life at all). The theoretical problem with supposing so is that we would then have no good reason to think that our perspective on the universe has any special merit. Suppose it is true: there is nothing special about the form of life that is, identically, rational life and humanity. Nothing in the nature of things requires that such a form exists; there is no correspondence between that form and the nature of things. But how then can there be any correspondence between the world itself and the lived world of humankind? Our lived world is only one, unpredictable and contingent, issue of the one real world within which all creatures have their day. Why should our world be 'truer' than the lived worlds of the sheep tick, bee or armadillo?

> We may, if we like, by our reasonings, unwind things back to that black and jointless continuity of space and moving clouds of swarming atoms which science calls the only real world. But all the while the world we feel and live in will be that which our ancestors and we, by slowly cumulating strokes of choice, have extricated out of this, like sculptors, by simply rejecting certain portions of the given stuff. Other sculptors, other statues from the same stone! Other minds, other worlds from the same monotonous and inexpressive chaos! My world is but one in a million alike embedded, alike real to those who may abstract them. How different must be the worlds in the consciousness of ant, cuttlefish or crab![21]

If intellect means anything, it must be a real response to a real world that privileges that response. Either we are as unprivileged as Gould suggests, or we are not. But if we are, we seem to have no reason to think that the world we live by sense or intellect (which is only another natural faculty) is anything much like the real world. It was difficult enough to believe that ordinarily selective processes could produce a truth-discovering being. If there was no selective process that produced us, but the chance of violent earthquakes, or a randomly mutated virus, at a crucial moment, we might as well expect ouija boards to work. I grant that it is conceivable that they do, as it is also conceivable that 'the patterns of badger-bone marrow give all the highway maps of the worlds.... If the whole universe were destroyed it could be reconstructed pretty nearly from the patterns of rock-badger bone-marrow.'[22] I simply can't see why this should be true, and therefore decline to believe it is. If that is so, we have no reason – in particular – to believe in this or any other reconstruction of the Burgess Shale.[23] If we have such reasons, then we must suppose – in reason – that the rational life is truer to the real world than any available other, and that there is something that explains such a conjunction (as neither evolutionary fitness nor chance survival does).

What is that rational life? One easy answer is that it involves a rigorous self-discipline, to cut us off from 'merely emotional' entanglements, so that we endorse only what can be established from accepted premises by logical demonstration or well-founded inference. The dream of reason begets monsters – or machines. On this account machines (whatever they may be built of) are Nature's mirror. Since the claim cannot be demonstrated, logically or inferentially, we are at liberty to disbelieve it utterly. Process-thinkers are at one with feminists, and with followers of the perennial philosophy (like me), in reckoning that rationality had better be considered an aspect of personal being. Logic and good inference alike are founded in personal honesty, in the wish to communicate on equal terms with all who can contribute. Only certain kinds of social group sustain the life of reason as it should be lived, and it is those that best embody the life that is called to mirror reality. Traditionalists call it love.

The word is slippery. The mutual recognition, comfort and applause that goes by the name of love may be a romantic dream, founded in lust and parent–child affection and the need for allies in a dangerous world. In its extremes personal affection is a rebellion against a world, physical or social, that does not go our way. It would be quite wrong to ignore its dangers and corruptions. But maybe we can also agree that in such love we seem to find a meaning, seem to touch the highest that we can conceive. God is that form of thinking that we know but rarely, and but for a moment, but He is forever. Aristotle intended by that aphorism to identify the contemplative love of what must be, although he also emphasized that it was with friends that we could best remember it. Enlightenment tradition chose either the intellect or the will as the focus of our presumed likeness to God. We grow more like God by understanding (too often equated with 'objectivist understanding') or by liberation from constraint. To be godlike is to be the master. One of Plotinus' errors was perhaps to suppose that Pheidias' statue (of a majestically bearded man) was what Zeus would look like if he took flesh.[24] Maybe the simplicity of love is indeed a better image, and He would look like the crucified, or like a child at play. 'Dear friends, let us love one another, because love is from God. Everyone who loves is a child of God and knows God, but the unloving know nothing of God. For God is love.'[25] The difference between John and Aristotle is perhaps less than we think. The love that John depicts is like and yet unlike our animal affections (and certainly very unlike the sticky and chaotic drooling that we too often think love is). The intellectual joy of Aristotle is not just higher physics. Both find eternal life in turning away from mortal matters, in realizing in themselves the eternal love of God (the love with which God loves, not that by which He is loved). 'In such a moment of discovery, we find that we have an interest in reality as such.'[26]

There is one way of reading this account that fits quite well with earlier remarks about evolution, and the powers of the scholastic God. If humanity (the kind and not the species) fulfils its part by revealing and delighting in the cosmos, then there is a sense in which the form of things is incarnate in humankind. If the rest of the world exists 'for us' and we exist to reflect it, then we could as easily say that we exist 'for it'. If what is important about humanity is that it can see outside itself to something more important, then the whole does not exist simply to give us something big to think about! It exists for its own sake. No god worth worshipping *needs* to deploy a universe to create its saints, but it might create a universe for its own sake, and saints to admire it. The conclusion almost has to be that the expanse of space and time, and all things in it, exist for their own sake, that they are – in a God's-eye-view – ends in themselves, not merely means to us. In the first place, God needs no such means (though Mega-Big might do so); in the second place, far too much of the universe, far too much even of the earth, is wholly irrelevant to our coming-into-being for that to be the only goal; in the third place, the experience of personal, reasoning life reveals the world as something to be valued for itself. We can suppose that one of the maker's goals is a world reflected in its parts, and especially in such parts as can achieve a personal, reasoning life. We cannot suppose that only those latter parts are wanted for themselves.

The danger is that even this vision is corruptible. We are special because we can see past our own small world, and learn to know and love the cosmos as something greater than our little lives. We are special because God gives us the whole world to rejoice in, not only a world specific to one smaller kind. If He has given it to us He must love us more. So we needn't pay any real attention to our fellow-creatures, beyond acknowledging them as part of God's great picture show. We must be being prepared for something better, when He shall make another heaven and earth for us to live in without older toys. And so the image, born in attentive love of the real cosmos, becomes another excuse for us to ignore it all, in favour of a fancy. That is the message of much liberal theology: without us the world would lose its point (because there'd be no one to know about it); all that is is really made for us, so as to give us clues and working metaphors for God. To this we must retort again that God as philosophical and Abrahamic tradition saw Him has no need of us, and the process-god has never told us what he wants. There is still no reason to believe that we are quite so special.

> What justifies the totally disproportionate cost of our presence? Ask it for once without presupposing the answer of the egotism of our species, as God might ask it about his creatures: why should a dog or a guinea pig die an agonizing death in a laboratory experiment so that some human need not suffer just such a fate?[27]

Is it our capacity for love that justifies unloving treatment of those whom we exclude from God's companionship? Are we so sure that what we practise is the more like love the less it is like anything they feel?

Maybe Blake was right to think that everything was summed up in the One Man, the Divine Imagination, that 'all deities reside within the human breast'. It does not follow that Metz was right to say that there is no world outside humanity,[28] because Blake's image is from the perennial philosophy, not anti-realist fantasy. The Man is equivalent, as in Philo of Alexandria, to the Word of God. We are human, by this account, in partly resembling Him, and He is the source and pattern of creation. It does not follow that everything is for us. That would be as absurd as claiming for human fathers all the worship due to God merely because God is our original Father, from whom all others get their name. Or deifying (or more likely killing) sheep because the Word is also the one Lamb, slain from before the foundation of the world. It is because God is Father that we should call no man by that name; because God is King that no one else can be; because God is His own first sacrifice (in making way for genuinely other beings) that no other sacrifice is needed, or permitted.[29]

## D Pyramids of sacrifice

Why emphasize the possible corruption of this branch of process theological thought? After all, in so far as it identifies what matters in us as the capacity for loving attention, it must help to focus it upon the creatures with whom we share, 'fellow-travellers' and 'fellow-creatures'. That theologians continue to speak as if we are the only goals God has is surely oversight. The trouble is that the vision is not egalitarian. Those who employ the insights of process theology to ground concerns for animal well-being or ecological integrity have begun to extend the bounds of the personal life, the love, they praise. As panpsychists they should certainly concede that such personality, such love is not entirely alien to other creatures. If they don't under-stand God, love or our endeavours as we do, they may still them-selves be loving (how much do we understand ourselves?). If they are not, we still know that, having the chance, we must be. But though this recognition of a wider world is welcome, process theologians remain convinced that a 'biocentric egalitarianism' is wrong. We must have more respect for 'richness of experience' and individual selfhood because we need criteria to prefer dogs to ringworms, and people to chickens.[30] Our vision, we are told, should be of 'a healthy biotic pyramid with man [sic] at its apex'.[31] 'God does not manifest Himself to an equal degree in everything':[32] guess where?

The criterion of 'richness' I find obscure. Cobb himself uses it to excuse an automatic preference against unborn children. Others have used it to divert resources away from the physically and mentally disabled – a strategy roundly condemned by recent writers with actual experience of the disabled. It is at least an interesting assump-tion (how would you prove it?) that the average middle-class human academic has a 'richer', more intense or more harmonious experience than the average domestic cat or woolly monkey. Modern biologists are far less obsessed with pyramids or trees, with 'man at the apex'. My own suspicion is that a 'healthy biotic pyramid', at best, means only that every individual has enough to breathe, eat, drink as long as it lasts (which may not be very long) and nothing gets eaten by an individual with a 'poorer' sense-experience. Some people influenced by this appear to find the existence, say, of bird-eating spiders more offensive than that of spider-eating birds, and moralistically con-demn 'man-eaters'. My further suspicion is that the criterion of rich-ness (since we cannot actually apply it) will turn out in practice simply to excuse the old familiar hierarchy: men, women, children (especially if they are civilized), dogs and cats and horses, donkeys and other 'higher' mammals, 'lower' mammals (as long as they aren't rats), birds, fish and reptiles, creepy-crawlies, vermin and the rest. And a special thank-you for what 'kills all known germs'. In brief the attempt to justify human pre-eminence by talking about the richness and intensity of our personal lives will end up by excusing all the old ways.

The image of the pyramid deserves one further gloss. The overt symbolism is doubtless of an Egyptian pyramid, and no more is meant than the familiar hierarchical illusion, that 'higher' must mean fewer. But there are other, more appropriate pyramids: the stepped pyramids of Babylon or the Aztecs. One of the revealing oddities of a 'creation spirituality' that harks back to the supposedly enlightened attitudes of 'Native Americans' is Barry Lopez's view of Tenochtitlan as 'the most beautiful city in the world'.[33] When environmentally conscious Christians use such phrases as 'the world's high priest' to identify a special role for *us*, we may remember, as before, what high priests did. We have often chosen to believe that we somehow did God service by slaughtering His creatures, or somehow even released their life, which is the blood, to Him. Perhaps these were the only terms on which we could feel easy about killing and eating them. We should not so readily indulge that thought by pretending to be the mediators between God and His world.

> Your countless sacrifices, what are they to me? says the Lord. I am sated with the whole-offering of rams and the fat of buffaloes. I have no desire for the blood of bulls, of sheep and of he-goats. . . . Though you offer countless prayers, I will not listen. There is blood on your hands . . . Put away the evil of your deeds, away out of my sight. Cease to do evil and learn to do right, pursue justice and champion the oppressed; give the orphan his rights, plead the widow's cause.[34]

Nor can any half-way objective eye be very impressed by talk of 'stewardship' when that is used to justify what we do. Better a steward, maybe, than a simple pirate – but what else did pirates ever do when they grew tired of travel or the treasure-ships were few? The origin of political society, in historical fact, was not in the free compact of equals, but in forced bargains whereby brigands settled down to farm instead of forage. To secure their status, and prevent the outbreak of rash sentiment among their young, they claimed to be God's messengers, and built pyramids.

This is a form of religion. Some claim, with reason, that it is the form of all religion. A Pharaonic world-state might employ just this religious rhetoric. The New Pharaoh would be head of GEA, and serve the varied peoples of the earth as god-with-us. Those peoples would be told that they all had their tasks, and must complete them so as to serve the land, the gods, the nobler classes (self-dedicated to a nobler service) and the Pharaoh. The more cynical amongst us might suspect deception – but it might well be true that the officers of GEA seriously believed that they were servants, stewards, well qualified to judge the relative richness of experience of the creatures whom they tamed, sincerely convinced that what they wanted were necessities, and what those lower wanted were indulgences. As now: tribesmen can be forbidden to hunt in national parks; if those of a higher class or caste found that they 'needed' something from those parks the rules would change.

> When the villagers go into the forest to get timber for their own personal needs they know that they are breaking the law but on the other hand, when these same villagers are hired by officials to fell trees and saw them up for timber for sale, then no laws are being broken![35]

The ancient Pharaonism was most concerned to maintain an unchanging realm, the gift of Nile. GEA's remit will be to conserve, but – if it adopts the ideology I have described – it will also think of change, of guided change. People as they are are bridges to a higher form, justified (as other species have been) by being the means to greater. The older humanism held that people, being rational persons, were 'ends in themselves'; the other picture of our station that I have teased out is that all things are 'ends', not merely means; the thought that is central to mainstream process-thought is that all things are means.

The moral is that there are religious forms which might help to moderate the carelessness with which we have assaulted our terrestrial home, and might even provide an ideology for the world-state that some think we need. It may well prove an attractive one, but mostly for reasons that do not sit well with deeper environmental values, or with liberal ones. It appeals because it denies an Absolute, because it fits our dreams of progress, because it gives us central billing in a story of the world, because it allows us still to do to animals and nature what we don't want to stop, because it's just what GEA needs. I doubt if it is what Gaia needs, or humankind.

## E The Sabbath

So what is the point of creation? 'The crown of creation is not the human being; it is the Sabbath.'[36] The Sabbath may be many things, but its meaning here is well explored by Kohak. The world of human interactions, even those more subtle interactions that are embodied as historical associations, is not the end. 'The world of my daily doings is a world structured by my active presence, and unintelligible it seems without it. . . . The most powerful realization that stands out in the dusk is that *all this is not so*.'[37] Occasionally, when we lay down our 'deadly doings',[38] things emerge as more than tools, materials or reminders. 'The Sabbath . . . a day of thanksgiving. Not the absence of activity, the act of honouring, or giving thanks is what restores the human soul and puts it at peace.'[39] The Sabbath as a Day of Creation sums up the various worlds: in it all things are at peace, no longer tools or material or self-serving individuals. 'This curious world we inhabit is more wonderful than convenient; more beautiful than it is useful; it is more to be admired and enjoyed than used.'[40] Even as a civil institution, of course, the weekly day of rest, for all within the family, freeborn or slave, human or non-human, is of enormous importance. In it limits are laid down on what may justly be demanded of our servants and ourselves. But the point is not only or at all a humanitarian one. The land itself must be allowed its Sabbaths: the wild things do not rest maybe, but they are released from human demands on them.

> To meet the Sabbath let us go
> From which the springs of blessing flow;
> Last of all creation wrought,
> First in God's primeval thought.[41]

This sixteenth-century Jewish hymn to the Sabbath Bride is not just an effusion to a familiar festival. It identifies the Sabbath, symbolically, as the Bride, the chronological equivalent of Zion, who is also the Bride.

> Rouse up, rouse up, behold thy light!
> Arise and shine, awake, awake!
> Thou art with God's own glory bright;
> With Song let all the mountains shake.
> Be not ashamed, be not aghast;
> Why art bowed down, disquieted?
> Their hope in thee the poor hold fast;
> Yea, ruined Zion shall lift her head.
> Despoilèd shall the spoiler be,
> Thine enemies scattered far and wide;
> Then shall thy God rejoice in thee
> As the bridegroom in the bride.

It was no new, sixteenth-century thought. The hope, the promise of Israel was of a people and a land united.

> No longer are you to be named 'Forsaken',
> Nor your land 'Abandoned',
> But you shall be called 'My Delight'
> And your land 'The Wedded';
> For Yahweh takes delight in you

> And your land will have its wedding.
> Like a young man marrying a virgin,
> So will the one who built you wed you,
> And as the bridegroom rejoices in his bride,
> So will your God rejoice in you.[42]

We may glimpse that resolution 'in the twilight', but it is not here-now. When it comes,

> the wolf lives with the lamb, the panther lies down with the kid, calf and lion cub play together with a little boy to lead them. The cow and the bear make friends, their young lie down together. The lion eats straw like the ox. The infant plays over the cobra's hole; into the viper's lair the young child puts his hand. They do no hurt, no harm on all my holy mountain, for the country is filled with the knowledge of Yahweh as the waters swell the sea.[43]

There is a tendency amongst modernists to allegorize this dream, as though Paul should be taken as authoritatively denying that 'God cares for oxen'. There is a similar trend amongst Buddhists, busily interpreting Gautama's earlier lives, and the Mahayana's hopes for universal enlightenment, as only marginally to do with the non-human. I prefer to believe that Isaiah (and the Mahayana) mean it.

The crown of creation is the Sabbath, or the new Jerusalem, the eternal fact continually passing through the fallen world and destined to absorb us into it. The world around us is not an arbitrary device merely to produce new people, of service to them in their long-drawn adolescence. Conceived in one way, temporally, it will one day be transformed, transfigured, and struggles till that time. Conceived in another, as the image of eternity, it is the fragmented and distorted copy of eternal wisdom – and for that reason no one fragment of it should be disowned or patronized or damaged. Platonist and Israelite alike can agree that God's concern is with the whole creation, and that belonging 'to the Kingdom of Heaven and His righteousness we can no longer be primarily children of nature or primarily children of civilization'.[44] Neither predation nor stewardship are proper models for us. Friendship may serve, as long as it is not confined to those we consider 'persons'.[45] 'We may treat Nature not as an object to conquer and turn wantonly to human service but as a *friend* [which is not to say a client or a lower servant] or a fellow being who is destined like ourselves for Buddhahood.'[46] Indeed, I would rather say, to be the bride.

There is no doubt that the Hebrews were lovingly aware of God's other creatures. The Torah and Rabbinic commonplace lay down the elementary rules of decency for dealing in hard times with wild and domestic creatures and with the land herself. Until the seventeenth century cruelty to animals was nowhere illegal, except in Jewish law, and in the long-defunct regulations of Asokan Buddhism. The claims of other creatures to the land we use were intimated in the Torah, and we were warned that if we did not respect those claims the land would be taken from us, and enjoy her Sabbath. All creatures seek their lives and livelihood from God, and He allows all things their turn, granting no special licence to human beings. God's grandeur is like mountains and the forest trees. It is He, and not impersonal Nature, that give things their bounds and their capacities together.[47] To suppose that the God of Israel tells us to despoil or to torment the creatures He sustains is, bluntly, illiterate. We are meant to wake up to their reality, and respect them as being real.

But though the God of Israel, or the Hebrews themselves, cannot sensibly or sanely be blamed for advising cruelty or carelessness to the land, it is certainly true that there is a long tradition in the West which looks askance at animals, and zoophiles – partly because the latter are suspected of being the sort of dreamers I have just deplored. Those who care, or say they care, for animals are regularly reckoned sentimentalists, averse to proper human relationships and probably perversely interested in the activities we share with animals.[48] Those who use these arguments rarely think them through – unlike Spinoza. If it is truly wrong to care for animals or for the land because these represent our merely material natures, we should not care much for our own material comforts. Such true ascetics, with their eyes fixed on their goal, would not disturb or traumatize their fellow creatures for material gain, even if they did not devote much energy to helping others to material gain. Those who care for their own comforts cannot without hypocrisy contend that others' comforts do not count at all. As it happens true ascetics usually do mind about the material lives of others, and show them a touching gentleness – like an antique philosopher who cares for his wards' property on the ground that they might need it if they don't turn out to be philosophers themselves. What makes Spinoza's charge not wholly silly is that people so readily deceive themselves that they are *caring* when they are only talking as if they care.

It is easy enough to quarry fine poetry from the Hebrew scriptures; almost as easy to uncover partial parallels between great traditions. What does it all amount to? 'A sentence uttered makes a world appear where all things happen as it says they do'[49] – and that is often

enough to satisfy us. If we have briefly *imagined* a better world, that
is as much as to make it, and we need trouble ourselves no longer
about our action or inaction in a dangerous world. Little else can
explain the way in which so many earnest believers, especially at
conferences about the duties of 'stewardship', *talk* lovingly about
God's creatures and the everlasting covenant, and then start eating
them.The thesis that Jewish, or Christian, doctrine is uniquely or
uniformly hostile to the claims of animals and nature is simply false
(though several doctors of the Church have borrowed unwisely from
older, mostly Stoic sources). But experience does, unfortunately, suggest that conferences of Christian theologians have a far lower proportion of active zoophiles than can now be expected at secular
conferences of philosophers.[50] A partial explanation is the general,
and not wholly discreditable, conservatism of the traditionally
religious. But this, and the residual effects of Stoic dogma, are not the
whole story. Even people who speak sincerely, and even movingly, of
God's love for all creation, appear to find no difficulty in financing
oppression, and feeding off the very creatures that they call their kin.
It is apparently felt unnecessary to do more than *say* these things
because the world of imagination 'in which we shall live in our
Eternal or Imaginative Bodies when these Vegetable Mortal bodies
are no more'[51] is so much more real.

The world of imagination: that is, of course, the criticism that so
many have made of 'religion', that it positively encourages us to live
as if in a dream, neglectful of 'real' duties. I have tried instead to
speak of religion as an instrument for 'waking up' from dream, from
the ordinary, sensual life. That, I believe, is what it has been meant to
be, and what in its various kinds, it often is. But any such waking
from what is immediately and attractively present requires us to
*imagine* ourselves within another world (even if it is only the world
of scientific myth). That world must then become more 'real' to us
than the everyday, whether it is filled with stars, or battles, or the
passage of Ra through the twelve hours of night. This sort of dualism, whatever the content of the imagined world, is likely to divert
attention from the everyday even when that is where we should in
fact be living. Dualism, I hasten to add, cannot be essentially misguided: if it were we should be forever stuck in whatever dream had
first been built around us. But waking to an imagined world that
does not draw the everyday world after it is hardly an improvement.
We say, or sing, a world in which we do not actually live, just as we

may turn from heartfelt prayer for spouse or child or colleague to abusing them.

Humanism has its merits, as has inhumanism. Humanists attempt to engage their wandering attention in a (reformed) everyday, a life lived by grown-up people. Inhumanists attempt 'a shifting of emphasis from man to not-man; the rejection of human solipsism and recognition of the trans-human magnificence'.[52] The former reminds us that the magnificence of present nature may corrode the heart – either because we do let our everyday affairs be moulded by that dream or because we don't. There are demands, they insist, which are not met in nature: 'nature' practises objective liability, but we should not; 'nature' is careless of the individual and of the type. Inhumanists point out in turn that those who think themselves *better* than the world, acquainted with a higher moral standard, too often prove to fall below the virtue of those they affect to despise. Believing others to be savages, we treat them savagely. Having hurt others beyond bearing we pretend that they *deserve* ill-fortune, that they are enemies of God, or that God is indifferent to their case. In which case we must be God's friends, and licensed to use the power we invest in a god stained by our image. 'He who boasts of the dignity of his nature and the advantages of his station, and thence infers his right of oppression of his inferiors, exhibits his folly as well as his malice.'[53]

But malice aside, there are still moral and metaphysical problems here. What moral duties do we really have if we are only part of the land that God is gathering to Himself, and if we must abandon the obscure and dangerous criterion of 'richness of experience'? Must 'biocentric egalitarianism' rule? And if it does, how can we avoid absurdity? My body, after all, which counts as only one amongst unnumbered many, is itself a colony organism, and each constituent cell must count for as much as the whole. If panpsychism is correct, each created unity is simultaneously one and many nested unities. Logically the only conclusion is that everything matters infinitely (since it is true only of infinities that every proper sub-set of a set has as many members as the whole[54]), but that is no clear guide when we are faced – as in this age we are – by questions of priority. Faced by two persons of equal moral dignity between whom we must choose (familiar cases concerning the deployment of scarce medical resources, for example) we must toss a coin, or offer some special reason why *this* person should be preferred, this time, to *that*. If we find ourselves invariably preferring this to that we should suspect our principles: no one should lose all the time. Must we also toss a coin when choosing between person, donkey, rat and the person's smallest cell? Maybe that is how a genuinely impartial God would rule – but He will hardly be surprised if we do not.

The conclusion might seem to be that we have, in practice, no alternative to the kind of prioritized, hierarchical structure that I have criticized before. Surely no large number of people will be convinced that they should treat cells and people equally, and even fewer will actually conform their everyday living to that particular fancy? But there is perhaps an alternative. The mistake that is made by those who criticize the egalitarian posture is to suppose that it has immediate implications for the dispersal of resources. It is compatible with human egalitarianism that we are not indifferent to particular people: we do not in fact treat people as interchangeable units (except in certain special cases). Rather we seek to ensure that every person (or rather, realistically, every fellow-citizen) has a roughly similar chance to live a life of her choosing, in company with others having a like chance. The goal of liberal humanism is not to be indifferent between people, but to ensure that no one class of person has such advantages or privileges as to make life not worth living, or not as well worth living, for any other class. The same system can be imagined for wider egalitarians: we should seek to act according to rules that allow all sorts of creature a fair chance of living a life of their choosing – which is the rule declared, in effect, to Job. This may, in this age of the world, imply that creatures are permitted to be predators, as long as there is some chance that their prey have lives too. Liberal egalitarians at least profess to allow behaviour that they themselves think wrong, so long as it is within the limits that could be agreed by all. Biocentric egalitarians can be tolerant too, though (like liberals) they may suddenly reach the limit of their forbearance. Like liberals they may perhaps be a little too optimistic about the prospects for a cheap and easy resolution of some conflicts, but it is a fault far smaller than the opposing view, that we can only resolve conflict by destroying the opposition. Much of this, if earlier remarks about the better ethical technique are right, must be left to concrete occasions and to careful agents, rather than being settled with a flourish of high principles.

The Sabbath is a moment when we are released to realize that everything is an end, not merely a means. From that perspective any further use we make of things must be conceived to be bounded by an imagined bargain, framed within the egalitarian rule I have described. I have yet to see any decent argument to defend our present uses of creation. 'Nothing was made by God for Man to spoil or destroy',[55] and all rightful appropriation of the land for our own purposes must leave as good for others. Locke intended, no doubt, to restrict the class of 'others' to the human, or even the civilized. Once that is recognized as superstition we must take greater care – in line with the commands of the Torah.


## F The uncreated world

Thus far the moral problem. The metaphysical is the old issue: what is the point of creation? The ancient philosophers, whether or not they took the notions of a creation or a definite beginning 'literally', had a simple answer. The cosmos was worth creating and could only be created because it embodied beauty, despite any real or apparent flaws in that embodiment. By one account the cosmos is an inevitable emanation from eternal Beauty, which needs no special reason to overflow or mirror itself in every realm of potential beauty. By another the cosmos is created to embody beauty because any good or reasonable creator will prefer to share and multiply that good. Inheritors of the Abrahamic tradition have chosen to emphasize God's freedom in creating, whereas purer Platonists have thought the event so certain as hardly to be creation at all, but rather emanation. The classes are not distinct. Consider Jonathan Edwards once again: 'a disposition in God, as an original property of His nature, to an emanation of his own infinite fulness, was what excited him to create the world.'[56] The contrast, for us, is not for now so important as the similarity. There is, after all, one feature of the cosmos that does not depend on any 'arbitrary' decision, namely the Word of God, the embodied Beauty. God does not create that Word, as though he might have created otherwise. Some details of its actual embodiment lie within His creative freedom, but it is in its essence 'begotten and not made'. This latter phrase is familiar from the Christian creed, but it is not an exclusively Christian notion.

All the faiths that trace their descent from Abraham have adopted the primary distinction between the One Incomprehensible Father and His Living Word, the pattern to which all things that have been made were made. The difference between these faiths lies in the presumed location of that Word: is it embodied in the Koran, considered as a text at once divine and earthly, or in the people of Israel around Mt Zion, or specifically as a Galilean *hasid*? Wherever it is is the real centre of creation. According to the Socino Chumash, the Rabbinic gloss on Genesis 1.31 (concerning the sixth day of creation) declares that 'the definite article is added [*the* sixth day] to teach that the whole of creation was dependent on the sixth day, viz. the sixth of Sivan, when Israel accepted the Torah; for had Israel rejected it, the universe would have been hurled back into its original nothingness'.[57] A similar tale is sometimes told of Mary's consent. In Rabbinic tradition God created the world, beginning with Zion.[58] This need not mean – though maybe it did – that Zion 'always' existed, however far back in the historical track we go. Maybe there was a time when Zion was not visible. It does not follow that the Zion in question was 'first' a bloodless blueprint, and only 'then' impressed on rock. The only Zion God made was that high city of Jerusalem, and 'then' – in the order of creation, not of our experience – invented a past history for its inhabitants. 'The mystery which reveals itself later in time than the appearance of men in the world comes before time itself in the dynamism of the making of all things.'[59] Similarly the Russian Platonist Bulgakov:

> In *Sophia* the fullness of the ideal forms contained in the Word is reflected in the creation. This means that the species of created beings do not represent new forms, devised by God, so to speak, *ad hoc*, but that they are based upon eternal, divine prototypes. For this reason therefore the world of creatures also bears a certain imprint of the world in God.[60]

The Sabbath, Zion or the incarnate Word can all be reckoned the real point, or even the beginning, of creation without it being necessary to think that the rest is only of instrumental value.

What matters here is the congruence between a Christian and an ordinarily Platonic incarnation of the Word. Christian theologians regularly say, of course, that Platonists, or maybe pagan Platonists, can have no notion of a true embodiment, but this is just a misunderstanding. Of course the Word can be embodied: that is the cosmos, a fractured vision of the divine order. The only question between pagan and Christian Platonist is whether it is the cosmos as a whole that necessarily embodies the Word, or whether it is some particular being. The Christian answer has been the latter, but of course no single being of the kind we actually see can exist without a cosmos. Any single being can, in a way, be thought of as the cosmos after one particular mode. If the Word is incarnate as one being among many its embodiment is as a universe. Conversely, if the Word is embodied as a cosmos, it is not every mode of that cosmos which properly identifies it as the living Word. There are, after all, corruptions and mistakes – or what we have to think so.

In so far as the world is what-should-be, the two worlds (of everyday and imagination) are united in the one true incarnation of the true and living word. There is something somewhere that is both the divine Word and entirely what could be expected in the natural world just there: it is, that is, both natural and divine. So what should it be? Where might the incarnation be? Even pagan philosophers, except the Stoics, did not contentedly suppose that the world should be entirely what, for experience, it is, or as it seems to be. Certainly Christians cannot revert to pantheism. We have to suppose that there is a way things should be (perhaps as defined by Isaiah), that they can be like that even if not through our own efforts, that what-should-be is somewhere acted out even if in a form constrained by the surrounding darkness. Denying the possibility of a true embodiment we gradually lose all sense that the cosmos even partially embodies what we can never know. Denying its actuality we deny that we or anyone else actually does know what should be. Insisting with orthodox Christians that Jesus actually is God's living word is saying that the world where Jesus is at home is the one world of which all other worlds are copies, fractured images, reminders. When Jesus was with the wild beasts in the desert he transformed our right relationships: what was on offer was a form of life detached from households, cities and productive labour. It is understandable that few of 'us' have ever been ready to accept that call: understandable, and perhaps correct. But it would do no harm for householders to recall how many great civilizations have elevated such a wanderer. The 'political life', as Aristotle said, is in the end a second best.

The 'theorizer', which is his preferred life, contemplates a truth, and – specifically – a truth that is worth contemplating, because it is beautiful. The theorizer, in brief, sees beauty, and may do so, Aristotle assured us, on the word of Herakleitos, in the most trivial-seeming circumstances. The relevant passage, from his *Parts of Animals*, is regularly quoted by working scientists, and can stand another citation:

> We must avoid a childish distaste for examining the less valued animals. For in all natural things there is something wonderful. And just as Heraclitus is said to have spoken to the visitors, who were wanting to meet him but stopped as they were approaching when they saw him warming himself at the oven – he kept telling them to come in and not worry 'for there are gods here too' – so we should

approach the inquiry about each animal without aversion, knowing that in all of them there is something natural and beautiful.[61]

There is an echo, doubtless deliberate, in Claude Bernard's more sinister observation, about 'the science of life [as] a superb and dazzlingly lighted hall which may be reached only by passing through a long and ghastly kitchen'.[62] Bernard missed Aristotle's point, that there was a real, discoverable beauty in the most trivial or even immediately disgusting things: a beauty to be acknowledged, even worshipped, and not torn apart to add a little detailed 'knowledge' to the library. Not every philosopher, despite Keats' rebuke, works to unweave rainbows or clip an angel's wings.[63] What matters to the kind of philosopher that Aristotle, and many others, praised is to fill her soul with the sight of beauty. There is another kind, whose aim is to master beauty, to remove its challenge by getting it in our power, by showing or pretending to show that it is nothing very special. Reductionist science of the kind that explains medium-sized objects and events by showing them to be the mathematical results of microscopic objects and events, need not have the reductionist effect of eliminating beauty. In fact, the reduction usually depends for its plausibility on the amazing beauty of the microscopic universe revealed as underpinning the universe of our immediate experience. But it may be that some such scientists really believe what is often said, that there is no 'real beauty' out there in the world, that it is only a projection of our aesthetic appetite upon a literally unmeaning realm of matter in directionless motion. What value there is in discovering such a 'truth' is more than I have ever seen, unless it is the familiar effort of the tailless fox to persuade his fellows that they would be better off de-tailed.

If there were no beauty to be discerned in nature it would not be worth discovering this.

> The scientist does not study nature because it is useful; he studies it because he delights in it, and he delights in it because it is beautiful. If nature were not beautiful, it would not be worth knowing, and if nature were not worth knowing, life would not be worth living.[64]

If nature were not beautiful, it would not even be possible to know it: as I remarked before, scientific theories about the unseen structure or forgotten past depend on our recognition of the subtle beauty of the mechanism involved. If there is no real beauty it is absurd to think one theory is more veridical because it is more beautiful. But the truth to which great scientists have testified is that Beauty is their firmest guide to truth. We can rely on that sense of beauty to lead us to the truth, because the truth is fixed by the demands of beauty. 'The plant is not in love with the Fibonacci series [which describe its stalk-production]; it does not seek beauty through the use of the golden section; it does not even count its stalks; it just puts out stalks where they will have the most room.'[65] But the order it unfolds or reveals is undoubtedly a real and powerful one, that is made known to us as beauty.

No one in this century has put the issue more eloquently than Simone Weil. 'The beauty of the world is the co-operation of divine wisdom in creation. . . . The object of science is the presence of Wisdom in the universe.'[66] She was also well aware of the temptation that beauty creates:

> It may be that vice, depravity and crime are nearly always, or even perhaps always, in their essence, attempts to eat beauty, to eat what we should only look at. . . . If [Eve] caused humanity to be lost by eating the fruit, the opposite attitude, looking at the fruit without eating it, should be what is required to save it.[67]

Does that seem absurd? If it does, it can only be because you see the only value of the fruit as instrumental, or wish to eliminate what might confront you with a more absolute demand. The impulse to use, to destroy, to humble what should be sacred to us has its effects elsewhere. Those who pride themselves on being 'practical' (in a lesser sense than Aristotle's) in effect deny the challenge that the beautiful presents. Nothing is worth admiring – except the products of their own determined efforts, and these not because they are beautiful but because they are their own. That is an understandable emotion – that is often how we love our children, after all – and one that should not be entirely dismissed. But admiring what we have done or made merely because we have done or made it is no recipe for a worthwhile life – because it isn't a recipe at all. More probably such practical people really see one form of beauty but neglect another: they may suggest that the conservationist's desire to maintain the beauty of a wood, or a cathedral, is only 'aesthetic preference' while themselves seeing the beauty (it may be the real beauty) implicit in the human endeavour to survive in spite of 'nature'. William James, walking through the woods, sees a forest made ulcerous by a squatter's hut 'without a single element of artificial grace to make up for the loss of Nature's beauty'. But the squatters see a personal victory, a living torn from the wilderness.[68] Noble deeds are beautiful as well, and human beings themselves, though they are not the most important entities, display the beauty that the theorizer loves. Someone living a worthwhile life has friends – precisely because such friends are beautiful, and do beautiful things (for noble deeds are 'noble' only because we are too shy to say they are beautiful, *kalai praxeis*).[69] Socrates was right to say that the sight of a beautiful boy could open our eyes, and right to say that physical consummation was a wrong response precisely because the lover would no longer think the boy was something still worth wondering at, nor would the boy benefit. Beauty is to be worshipped, and cannot be possessed.[70]

Practical virtue is exercised in doing what is beautiful, but it is the contemplatable beauty of the act that makes the exercise worthwhile. The beauty of ordinarily moral action is not the only beauty (and it is indeed a beauty possible only in a fallen world), but it is a manifestation of the quality the theorizer sees. That moral approbation comes under the same heading as aesthetic is a thought that has been out of fashion for many years,[71] partly – no doubt – because we have come to think that 'beauty' is only a projection, and fear to think the same of moral goodness. We have so far forgotten our past as to imagine that calling a character beautiful is only a strained metaphor. But Plotinus meant what he said.[72]

Perfect virtue is complete virtue, with every disposition well-proportioned, and the goal of action Beauty. Truly virtuous people, according to tradition, do not merely recognize natural goods as being good-for-them, and act accordingly. They act for the sake of the beautiful – not, that is, to benefit the beautiful, but to exemplify it, to give it an entry to the changing world. They act so as to be performing beautifully, whether their act must be to deal with ill-health and poverty, or with the natural goods.[73] Perfectly virtuous people act so as to embody in their character and conduct the ideal of sound, and lively, proportion that our evolution has constrained us to intuit, the beauty that Plotinus praised so largely.[74] This, traditionally, has been the ethical ideal: not simply to secure what is good-for-oneself as a healthy and harmonious human being, things like honour and friendship and a quiet life, but to do what is fine and noble, what is objectively required not simply for the good of the agent, but by the beauty of the act itself.

Both idealistic and non-idealistic hedonists, by putting the value of moral action in the imagined consequences of those acts, specifically the pleasures they perhaps engender, license oppression, and the alienation of value. Aristotle's conviction, shared by other ancient moralists, was that the value of moral action lay in its beauty, the self-same beauty that is displayed in the world's order, in well-built friendships and in well-built cities. The only final end is beauty, and the best life for human beings is to see and serve that beauty. Tactile pleasures and future achievements (valued for increasing tactile pleasures) are no sure basis for a worthwhile life. One question remains: is it better to build beauty or to worship its presence in the world (the world, that is, of stars, trees, flowers, beetles, horses, birds and people)? Is it better, in short, to be a citizen or a resident alien? Unless God keeps the house their labour is but lost that built it: unless, that is, the love of present beauty is alive there, the citizen works in vain (however many temples, courts and palaces she builds). But even if the citizen's labour is not vain it struggles against fearful odds. No one can ensure that someone else experiences the love of God, or lives by it, and even if the labouring citizen is confident that she lives with beauty her failure or possible failure to preserve the city must weigh on her. Because her hope is placed outside herself she must so act as to preserve some few who live in beauty more securely than she does.

Another, longer quote from Weil:

> We live in a world of unreality and dreams. To give up our imaginary position as the centre, to renounce it, not only intellectually but in the imaginative part of our soul, that means to awaken to what is real and eternal, to see the true light and hear the true silence. A transformation then takes place at the very roots of our sensibility, in our immediate reception of sense impressions and psychological impressions. It is a transformation analogous to that which takes place in the dusk of evening on a road, where we suddenly discern as a tree what we had at first seen as a stooping man; or where we suddenly recognize as a rustling of leaves what we thought at first was whispering voices. We see the same colours, we hear the same sounds, but not in the same way. To empty ourselves of our false divinity, to deny ourselves, to give up being the centre of the world in imagination, to discern that all points in the world are equally centres and that the true centre is outside the world, this is to consent to the rule of mechanical necessity in matter and of free choice at the centre of each soul. Such consent is love. The face of this love which is turned towards thinking persons is the love of our neighbour: the face turned towards matter is love of the order of the world, or love of the beauty of the world which is the same thing.[75]

Those who make no attempt to live 'in the presence of God' or (equivalently) 'in beauty' are not living worthwhile lives. Those who do will also seek to do their duty in the world, but will not imagine that their job is to 'improve' the world.

The really pessimistic view, which may be mainstream Platonism and certainly seems to be what modernists prefer, is that there will never be any real change. Whether or not there is a real unfallen world (as Platonists say there is and modernists deny) this world will always be the world it is. Chardinists may suggest that some day the world will be fully humanized, turned into the sort of leisure park that hedonism proposes. The claim seems at once wildly optimistic and deeply depressing. Other modernists only suggest that we should somehow make our personal lives endurable, accepting that the rest of the world is unredeemed and unredeemable. The best we can expect, in Aristotle's eyes, is to catch a glimpse of beauty from among the shadows. I suggest that the central Christian message, and that of other Abrahamists, is that the unfallen world will at last return. Muir commenting on the transfiguration:

> Was it a vision?
> Or did we see that day the unseeable
> One glory of the everlasting world
> Perpetually at work, though never seen
> Since Eden locked the gate that's everywhere
> And nowhere? Was the change in us alone,
> And the enormous earth still left forlorn,
> An exile or a prisoner?[76]

He seems to have answered his question that the unfallen world is there, and that we shall one day find a transformation, an awakening

> For all things,
> Beasts of the field, and woods, and rocks, and seas,
> And all mankind from end to end of the earth
> Will call him with one voice.

If that is so, and the land will have – does have – its place in that world renewed, we must acknowledge that the land and its denizens here-now cannot be treated solely as property, claimed or unclaimed. When that day comes, how shall we face them?

# Notes

1. S. Weil, *Notebooks*, tr. A. Wills (Routledge & Kegan Paul: London, 1956), vol. I, p. 241.

2. J. Hick, *Evil and the God of Love* (Fontana: London, 1968).

3. P. Anderson, 'Epilogue' in *Time and Stars* (Gollancz: London, 1964), pp. 119–80; see also R. Rucker, *Infinity and the Mind* (Paladin: London, 1984), pp. 180ff, after J. von Neumann.

4. B. McKibben, *The End of Nature* (Penguin: Harmondsworth, 1990), p. 163.

5. This is of course the argument that Dawkins uses against theism: *The Blind Watchmaker* (Longman Scientific & Technical: Harlow, 1986). It applies to the world-engineer but not to the God of orthodox tradition, who is not complex.

6. Steven Jay Gould, *Wonderful Life: The Burgess Shale and the Nature of History* (Penguin: Harmondsworth, 1991: first published by Hutchinson, 1989). For further discussion see my 'Does the Burgess Shale have moral implications', *Inquiry* 36 (1993).

7. Gould, *Wonderful Life*, p. 35. See also G. G. Simpson, 'The non-prevalence of humanoids', *Science* 143 (1964), pp. 769–75.

8. O. Stapledon, *Last and First Men* (Penguin: Harmondsworth, 1972), p. 119. The major oddity of Stapledon's fables to a later eye is that he expected history to move so slowly.

9. See T. Wilder, *The Bridge of San Luis Rey* (Longmans, Green & Co.: London, 1941).

10. Gould, *Wonderful Life*, pp. 294ff.

11. Gould, ibid., p. 297.

12. Gould, ibid., p. 310.

13. Gould, ibid., p. 318.

14. Gould, ibid., p. 320.

15. Gould, ibid., p. 291.

16. S. Weil, *The Need for Roots*, tr. A. F. Wills (Ark Paperbacks: London and New York, 1987), p. 164. This is not to say that we cannot wish our friends immortal.

17. See my 'Is humanity a natural kind?' in T. Ingold (ed.), *What Is an Animal?* (Unwin Hyman: London, 1988), pp. 17–34, and 'Apes and the idea of kindred' in P. Singer and P. Cavalieri (eds), *The Great Ape Project* (Fourth Estate: London, 1993), pp. 113–25.

18. See my *Aristotle's Man* (Clarendon Press: Oxford, 1975), p. 25.

19. Gould, *Wonderful Life*, pp. 321ff.

20. Gould, ibid., p. 292.

21. W. James, *The Principles of Psychology* (Macmillan: London, 1890), vol. 1,

pp. 288f.; see my *From Athens to Jerusalem* (Clarendon Press: Oxford, 1984), pp. 133ff.

22. R. A. Lafferty, *Arrive at Easterwine* (Ballantine Books: New York, 1973), p. 190.

23. See *Athens to Jerusalem*, pp.39f.

24. Plotinus, *Enneads* 1.8.1, 39–40.

25. 1 John 4.7f. (NEB).

26. O. O'Donovan and R. Grove-White, 'An alternative approach', p. 73, in R. Attfield and K. Dell, *Values, Conflict and the Environment* (Ian Ramsey Centre: Oxford, 1989), pp. 73–82.

27. E. Kohak, *The Embers and the Stars* (University of Chicago Press: Chicago, 1984), p. 92.

28. See J. B. Cobb, *Process Theology as Political Theology* (Manchester University Press: Manchester, 1982) p. 6.

29. See my *The Mysteries of Religion* (Blackwell: Oxford, 1986), pp. 162ff. for further remarks on 'sacrifice' as the necessary mode of creation.

30. J. B. McDaniel, *Of God and Pelicans* (Westminster/John Knox Press: Louisville, 1989), pp. 75, 79.

31. J. B. Cobb, *Is It Too Late?: A Theology of Ecology* (Bruce: Beverly Hills, 1972), p. 55.

32. J. Moltmann, *God in Creation*, tr. M. Kohl (SCM: London, 1985), p. 103, citing Heinrich Hesse (1835).

33. B. Lopez, *Crossing Open Ground* (Vintage Books: New York, 1989); cited by M. Fox, *Creation Spirituality* (Harper: San Francisco, 1991), p. 123.

34. Isaiah 1.11, 15f. (NEB).

35. A. Pongsak, 'In the water there were fish and the fields were full of rice', p. 89, in M. Batchelor and K. Brown (eds), *Buddhism and Ecology* (Cassell: London and New York, 1992), pp. 87–99.

36. Moltmann, *God in Creation*, p. 31.

37. Kohak, *Embers*, p. 73; see my *God's World and the Great Awakening* (Clarendon Press: Oxford, 1991), pp. 218ff.

38. There is an evangelical hymn, as I recall, including the line: 'Lay your deadly doings down – doing ends in death'.

39. Kohak, *Embers*, p. 81.

40. H. D. Thoreau, *Familiar Letters*, ed. F. B. Sanborn (Houghton Mifflin: Boston, 1894), p. 9; cited by W. Berry, *What Are People For?* (Rider Books: London, 1990), p. 138.

41. Shelomah Halevi Alkabetz (sixteenth century), tr. P. H., *Jewish Chronicle* (6 May 1898). A cutting from my family's past!

42. Isaiah 62.4f. (JB).

43. Isaiah 11.6ff. (JB).

44. H. Paul Santmire, *Brother Earth* (Thomas Nelson Inc.: New York and London, 1970), p. 132.

45. See S. McFague, *Models of God* (SCM Press: London, 1987).

46. D. T. Suzuki, cited by McDaniel, *God and Pelicans*, p. 97.

47. See P. Gregorios, *The Human Presence* (WCC: Geneva, 1978), p. 19.

48. B. Spinoza, *Ethics*, tr. S. Shirley, ed. S. Feldman (Hackett: Indianapolis, 1982), 4p37s1; see also 3p57, 4p68s.

49. W. H. Auden, 'Words' in *Collected Shorter Poems* (Faber: London, 1966).

50. A notable exception is of course Andrew Linzey: see *Christianity and the Rights of Animals* (SPCK: London, 1987).

51. W. Blake, *Jerusalem* §77 in *Complete Writings*, ed. G. Keynes (Clarendon Press: Oxford, 1966), p. 717.

52. R. Jeffers, *The Double Axe and Other Poems* (Liveright: New York, 1977), p. xxi.

53. H. Primatt, *The Duty of Humanity to Inferior Creatures* (Centaur Press: Fontwell, 1992; first published, ed. A. Broome, 1831), p. 22.

54. There are, for example, as many even numbers as there are numbers; there are also just as many multiples of a googol and seven ($10^{100} + 7$). So each cell of my body is worth just as much as me if every one of us is infinitely valuable.

55. J. Locke, *Two Treatises on Government*, 2.31, ed. P. Laslett (Cambridge University Press: Cambridge, 1963), p. 332.

56. J. Edwards (1755); cited by M. Sagoff, *Economy of the Earth* (Cambridge University Press: London, 1988), p. 133; see Moltmann, *God in Creation*, pp. 79ff.

57. *Socino Chumash*, ed. A. Cohen (Soncino Press: Hindhead, 1947), p. 7.

58. M. Eliade, *Cosmos and History*, tr. W. R. Trask (Harper & Row: New York, 1959), p. 16.

59. A. Squire, *Asking the Fathers* (SPCK: London, 1973), pp. 22f. after 1 Corinthians 15.45.

60. S. Bulgakov in J. Pain and N. Zernov (eds), *A Bulgakov Anthology* (SPCK: London, 1976), p. 154. I have discussed this apparently strange doctrine further in *God's World and the Great Awakening*, pp. 129ff.

61. Aristotle, *De Partibus Animalium* 1.645a15ff.tr. D. F. Balme (Clarendon Press: Oxford, 1972), p. 18 (see p. 123: 'possibly a polite euphemism for "visiting the lavatory" ' – which is also a euphemism).

62. Claude Bernard, *Introduction to the Study of Experimental Medicine*, tr. H. C. Greene (New York, 1949), p. 15; Bernard was the father of modern physiology, and an unrepentant vivisector who conducted many of his brutal experiments on dogs immobilized with curare.

63. J. Keats, 'Lamia' II, 229ff. in *Poetical Works*, ed. H. W. Garrod (Oxford University Press: London, 1956), pp. 176f.

64. H. Poincaré; cited by R. Weber, *Dialogues with Scientists and Sages* (RKP: London/Methuen: New York, 1986), p. xix.

65. P. S. Stevens, *Patterns in Nature* (Penguin: Harmondsworth, 1976), p. 166. M. Mothersill, *Beauty Restored* (Clarendon Press: Oxford, 1984), pp. 125 ff. discusses Fibonacci and the Golden Section, unsympathetically.

66. Weil, *Notebooks*, pp. 122, 124.

67. Weil, ibid., p. 121.

68. J. K. Roth (ed.), *The Moral Philosophy of William James* (New York, 1969), pp. 215f: James realizes the conflict, and attempts some resolution.

69. Aristotle, *Nicomachean Ethics* 9.1170a2ff.

70. See Michael McGhee, 'Chastity and the male philosopher', *Journal of Applied Philosophy* 10 (1993).

71. See G. Sircello, *A New Theory of Beauty* (Princeton University Press: Princeton and London, 1975), pp. 81ff.

72. Plotinus, *Enneads* I.6.4: tr. S. Mackenna (Faber: London, 1956), p. 59: the passage cited earlier (p. 70).

73. Aristotle, *Politics* 7.1332a20f.

74. See my 'Natural goods and moral beauty' in D. Knowles and J. Skorupski (eds), *Virtue and Taste: Essays on Politics, Ethics and Aesthetics in Memory of Flint Schier* (Blackwell: Oxford, 1993), pp. 83–97.

75. Weil, *Notebooks*, p. 115.

76. E. Muir, 'The Transfiguration', *Collected Poems* (Faber: London, 1960), pp. 199f.

........................................6

# The last things

...........................................

## A The debts of gratitude

I ended the last chapter with a poem of Edwin Muir's. Another poem
begins

> I am debtor to all, to all I am bounden,
> Fellowman and beast, season and solstice, darkness and light,
> And life and death.[1]

What we are, we owe to others. Traditionally, of course, our greatest
debt of gratitude must be to God: the difference between non-being
and being is infinite, and all the resources from which we might repay
the debt are at once finite and not ours to use. Either we receive
our being as a gift, from Chesterton's abyss of light, or we must
acknowledge an infinite indebtedness. Fox identifies the idea of 'gift'
as liberating, though the prose in which he does so is, to my ears,
sentimental.[2] From that first perspective none of us are wronged
whatever happens to us: we receive being as the beings that we are,
and cannot coherently make any complaint at all. This is indeed the
plea that some secular philosophers have used to excuse our lack of
care for the future: any later generations faced by a despoiled and
degraded landscape would not exist at all (those actual individuals
wouldn't) if we had not despoiled and degraded, and therefore could

not be any better off if we had behaved better. Even statesmen, I am glad to say, have resisted this:

> Over a hundred years ago John Ruskin wrote 'God has lent us the earth for our life. It is a great entail. It belongs as much to those who follow us as it does to us, and we have no right by anything we do, or neglect to do, to involve them in unnecessary penalties, or to deprive them of the benefit we have it in our power to bequeath.' This has a very contemporary ring to it. Nothing that I recall being said in Rio quite matched Ruskin's elegance and economy of expression. . . . The task before us now is to give practical expression to Ruskin's admonition, that is, to put sustainable development into practice.[3]

The same thought preceded Ruskin. The earth belongs in usufruct to the living, said Jefferson,[4] or rather is held in trust for the unborn. 'The land belongs to (God) and to (Him) we are only strangers and guests.'[5] If future generations should be glad to exist on any terms, then so should we – and not impose enormous costs on them in order ourselves to live a little better. The thought also preceded Jefferson. 'This is what an early Muslim legal scholar, Abu al-Faraj, says: People do not in fact own things, for the real owner is their Creator; they only enjoy the usufruct of things, subject to the Divine Law.'[6] And again, to one who had dug canals and reclaimed abandoned land: 'Partake of it with joy, so long as you are a benefactor, not a corrupter, a cultivator, not a destroyer.'[7]

So from an only slightly different point of view there are many who have a real complaint against us, in that their lives are lessened for our sake – and may be so even by 'sustainable development', as though one should decide to take no more slaves from Africa than the continent could sustainably supply. On the one hand the gift is infinite; on the other it is lessened by the acts and omissions of others. Not all our debts to others rest on those others' injuries: in some cases we have been benefited by what has benefited those others too. Our debts to them and theirs to us may balance out. They may balance out even if we do each other reciprocal injury: once the cycle of bloodshed is begun each new blood-letting is at once a fit response to an older crime, and a new crime demanding a requital. In the very beginning 'all things were tame and gentle to people, both beasts and birds, and their friendship burned bright'.[8] Empedocles mourned his own past sin, which had condemned him to suffer the same for thrice ten thousand years, 'an exile from the gods and a wanderer, having put his trust in raving strife'.[9]

The idea that some primordial sin has condemned us to the round of bloodshed, and the hope that in an eschatological 'ninth year'[10] we shall be restored to the sun above, are now denounced as dualism or misanthropy by liberal theologians. A real expectation of the Sabbath, a radical transformation of the present day, is bad enough. To condemn that present as punitive or purgatorial is variously labelled 'Gnostic', 'Manichaean' or, of course, Platonic. Good theists, we are taught to think, should think the world of nature good as it is, and should impute all real evils to the deliberate choice of individual people. The admitted pains and hardships of the world are justified as necessary educational devices for the production of good moral agents like ourselves, and neither punishments for any primal sin, nor sins themselves. Because we should not condemn the world of nature but think it good just as it is, nothing that we do in imitation of that nature is condemnable. Because the world of nature is admirable we may therefore seek to control, conquer and exploit that world. The converse thesis, that *pleonexia* is wrong, predatory exploitation not what God desires of us, identifies the world of predatory exploitation as something to be surpassed. It is all too easy to suppose that what we should surpass we are entitled to transform, and therefore to subject to predatory exploitation: witness the views attributed to Reagan's Secretary of the Interior, James Watt, that the present world is due to be transformed or abandoned at 'the Second Coming'.[11] The fallacy is the belief that such transformation is in our power to effect, or else in no one's. Really, Watt might as well have concluded that those human beings that cannot reform themselves might as well be abandoned to outright destruction. If God can redeem us, He can redeem the world: how could the redeemed forget the *old* Jerusalem?

The first moral must be that every theological doctrine is open to abuse, that we will find excuses for our own behaviour whatever it is we say we think. The second is to try and find a path between two major errors. One error is to love 'nature' as it is, and imitate it. Consider Philimore's parody of Coleridge's poem:

> He prayeth best who loveth best
> All things both great and small;
> And streptococcus is the test,
> I love him best of all.[12]

The second is to disapprove of nature. Loving the things there are, and hoping for their redemption, we must recognize much of what things do as evil. Chesterton's words are to the point:

Let us suppose that we are confronted with a desperate thing – say Pimlico. If we think what is really best for Pimlico we shall find the thread of thought that leads to the throne of the mystic and the arbitrary. It is not enough for a man to disapprove of Pimlico: in that case he will merely cut his throat or move to Chelsea. Nor, certainly, is it enough for a man to approve of Pimlico: for then it will remain Pimlico, which would be awful. The only way out of it seems to be for somebody to love Pimlico: to love it with a transcendental tie and without any earthly reason. If there arose a man who loved Pimlico, then Pimlico would rise into ivory towers and golden pinnacles: Pimlico would attire herself as a woman does when she is loved.[13]

It is not necessary for those who love the living earth to think that all things are exactly all right as they are: indeed it is necessary that they do not. Whatever vision of 'orient and immortal wheat' afflicts us, let us not forget the wild things we have excluded from those fields, the poisons we have spread on them, the prospect of soil erosion and decay. The immortal light will shine, no doubt, even in and on a land degraded and despoiled. The picture of a land 'defiled, diseased' that I quoted earlier could be rewritten. 'The world is charged with the grandeur of God',[14] whatever smells and smudges we have left on it: 'there lives the dearest freshness deep down things', even if it is, in some sense, hidden in the dust. Mordor itself persists because the rocks and fires maintain the nature they were given in the very beginning. To be at all, after all, is still to be *something*, and that Something is itself a form in the divine thought.

> The shepherds' hovels shone, for underneath
> The soot we saw the stone clean at the heart
> As on the starting day. The refuse heaps
> Were grained with that fine dust that made the world.
> For he had said, 'To the pure all things are pure'.[15]

This vision is available to those who 'praise the Lord', or practise whatever other ritual enables them to *thank*. Empowered by it, they may transform the heaps. That at least is essential to any 'new' religion.

## B Atonement

So what should someone do for Pimlico, and for the world, and what is love? Fox speaks of 'falling in love with a galaxy':[16] what does this mean? It is easy to say that someone should love (as it were) Pimlico 'without any earthly reason' and thereby assist it to be what Pimlico should be. But suppose that Pimlico's condition is in part a consequence of debt, blood-feud or self-tormenting guilt? Must not any transformation turn on redemption, judgement and forgiveness? And is it obvious that forgiveness can be quite easy? Soskice quotes a song of Joni Mitchell's ('Woodstock', 1969):

> We are stardust. Million year old carbon.
> We are golden. Caught in the devil's bargain
> And we've got to get ourselves back to the garden.

Soskice comments on the 'nascent Pelagianism' of the song, and adds that 'we are dust that has come to know itself as dust, to know that dust can do right and commit wrongs'.[17] That seems an important recognition, and one that non-Christian environmentalists should applaud. Those who attempt to revitalize Goddess-worship characteristically speak of a supposedly patriarchalist religion as violent and judgemental, but the Goddess of past mythology and future expectation is at least as violent. As Heine points out, it is Anat of Ugarit, not Yahweh, who wades with joy through the blood of her enemies.[18] The development of Rabbinic Judaism is towards a God who 'desireth not the death of a sinner'. A responsible ecofeminism must follow suit. But there remains a real value in the thought of judgement, even if it is sometimes pictured in appallingly inhuman ways. 'Consciousness of acute and humanly irremediable sin may create its own fantasies of punishment which it will be almost a relief actually to endure.'[19] The fantasy of giants' judging humanity, and brushing the rock clean,[20] or the earth's reacting against a species that has transgressed its natural limits, or a Galactic Empire's patronizing decision that we have 'lost touch with real life' and so deserve destruction, all crop up in the modern literary consciousness. Part of the time we fear that we have gone too far, and must expect retribution – as the Aztecs did.[21] Gray's insight: 'What bitter cruelty all of us exercise! Nothing that happens to me in future will I ever feel unjust and unmerited.'[22] Can we be reassured by the mere assertion that God's a good fellow and 'twill all be well? Does it help us live more sanely to believe that He is not?

Our fear and fantasy contradict the main thrust of the Enlightenment – that nothing happens in nature because of any particular 'moral value'. Disasters are not always caused by human sin, and are never simply punishment. That was indeed an older view as well: those who died when the tower of Siloam fell were no more sinners than the rest of us. Fear of judgement, and attempts to identify those judgements – especially on others – are consequences of our own pride. Because we insist on others' paying their trivial debts to us, we suppose that the Lord makes similar demands on us, unless we can somehow flatter Him into forgiving us our debts. If we believe ourselves successful, and that He has, by arbitrary judgement, let us off, we may perhaps, as the parable requires of us,[23] let others off, but are as likely, as the parable suggests, to demand prompt payment to those favoured of the Lord. If we are God's favourites and He will forgive us everything it is easy to conclude that we are at liberty to demand a proper respect from others. How else do royal favourites act? This may be one further explanation for the complacent sentimentalism that, I am afraid, hangs round some conventionally light green theologizing: it is enough to *say* that we appreciate God's grandeur, while happily eating up our feathered, finny and four-footed cousins – and 'the children of the Sahel'.[24] One message of the gospel is that we are *not* God's favourites, but forgiven on the express condition that we ourselves forgive, that we do not demand our rights. By giving up our lives we gain them; by seeking to maintain our lives and livelihood we lose them all.

> Forgive your neighbour the hurt he does you, and when you pray, your sins will be forgiven. If a man nurses anger against another, can he then demand compassion from the Lord? Showing no pity for a man like himself, can he then plead for his own sins? Mere creature of flesh, he cherishes resentment; who will forgive him his sins?[25]

The enterprise is a lot more difficult than the ritual commitment to forgiveness that our liturgies require. We had better, as a beginning, proclaim again 'the acceptable year of the Lord', the Jubilee, and forgive all Third World debts.[26] Until we do, our 'gratitude' is sentimental.

Suppose that we can be assured of God's forgiveness on the one condition that we forgive those who are in our debt, that we do not require of them what, in a sense, we do have a right to require. Are our debts then forgiven, and no reparations necessary? Even this much is hardly reassuring. Maybe mendicants and eremites, receiving in sheer gratitude whatever happens, may feel themselves at peace with God, but you and I are householders and citizens. We check our bills, and safety-lock our windows, dislike queue-jumpers and resent too frequent calls upon our time and patience. But suppose, somehow, we did forgive our debtors. Would that be enough? It is not clear that it could be. If God were my only creditor, then I would be entirely at His mercy. I cannot pay the debt of being except by an infinite service; cannot pay, equivalently, except by forgiving everything I'm owed. But as Muir said: 'I am debtor to all, to all I am bounden.' Maybe, as they hope for forgiveness they too should forgive, but how can I count on that? If they choose not to forgive, how am I forgiven? Can the Lord of the parable forgive his servant all the debts he owes to others? 'The transgressions of man toward God are forgiven him by the Day of Atonement; the transgressions against other people are not forgiven him by the Day of Atonement if he has not first appeased the other person.'[27]

Liberal Christian theologians are embarrassed by all doctrines of the Atonement (once a crucial feature of the Christian creed) save the exemplary. The sight of a good man, 'led like a sheep to the slaughter', may strip us of any admiration for the powers-that-be. If that is what the best of earthly authority produces, that best is not worth worship. *Mere* disillusionment might lead as easily to nihilism, but we may instead find love kindled in our hearts for the one whose execution disillusioned us. What we love instead of civil power and piety is the self-sacrificial love of one who walks clear-eyed to death to show us what the powers are really like. This too may be nihilistic in effect: what sort of love is it that seeks to disillusion us by compelling the powers to act unkindly, if no better life is offered us than the best we have yet devised? Do we gain by disillusionment? Would we thank someone who successfully showed the one we loved in a bad light (by goading her to acts she might herself regret)? Either we would forswear all love because we had been deceived, or else we would forgive the one we'd loved, knowing her but mortal. Only if the disillusioner somehow revealed herself as worthier of love, would we transfer our affections. The story is not impossible. An exemplary 'atonement' can only be the demonstration of a way of life more admirable than any other, even in its destruction. The just man vilified and impaled is still to be preferred to the successfully unjust, as Plato said.

Christ's gift to us, on this account, is only what any martyred saint may give: the reassurance or alarming realization that it is possible to live and die in grateful obedience to the Lord – the Lord, that is, of Justice, not the powers-that-be. Those who seek to defend their lives will lose them, or lose what really makes their lives worthwhile. Guarding the little flame of generosity within our hearts requires us to go without complaint where we are led, owning and demanding nothing. It is, to state the obvious again, a more alarming prospect than we usually admit. Achieving anything resembling it requires more love, more trust than most of us can manage.

The exemplary model lends little support to doctrines of Christ's uniqueness, or the need for such a death. At most it may excite us just a little more, and provide a ritual and vocabulary to channel our emotions. At best it is just a little less deconstructible than other exemplary deaths, from Socrates to Bhutto. Such deaths disillusion and inspire, but quickly raise new questions: what did the martyr really witness to, and would we live likewise even if we could? If Christian incarnational faith is not simply to be deconstructed in favour of a renewed monotheism resembling Islam, or even of a post-Christian humanism, the exemplary model has to be enhanced. It is atonement theory that is the distinctively Christian contribution to an environmentally conscious piety.

If our debts are to be forgiven, it is our creditor who must release us. If God forgives me my infinite debt to Him on the express condition that I release my debtors, I may perhaps succeed in doing so, and yet still be in debt. Those other creditors have their own debts to pay, and may also achieve God's forgiveness by releasing me. But suppose they don't: they are then unreconciled to God, but not therefore without some rights of their own. Maybe they should, for their souls' sake, forgive, as so should I. But are my debts to them wiped out because they remain God's debtors? It would be a pleasant thought, perhaps, if it were so. Stoic argument identified the wise as friends of God and thence concluded that, since friends have all things in common and the world is God's, all things belong to the wise. Whatever they take they need not pay for, as it is theirs already. It is necessary, for the Stoics' credit, to add at once that no Stoic identifies herself as wise, and that the wise display their wisdom by making no destructive claims on things. If wise, I 'own' the world by not exploiting it. Maybe the saints of God have as strong a claim on us as God Himself, and therefore have no creditors at all, but we aren't saints, and even saints don't claim to own the world in any sense that wholly denies the debts they may have incurred before their saintliness set in.

How then can we be forgiven the debts our creditors do not choose to forswear? By not forgiving those debts the creditors act out the part of Satan, the accuser, and exclude themselves from reconciliation.

The Gibeonites who lacked pity [2 Samuel 21] put themselves outside Israel. . . .

The Talmud teaches that one cannot force men who demand retaliatory justice to grant forgiveness. It teaches us that Israel does not deny this imprescriptible right to others. But it teaches us above all that if Israel recognizes this right, it does not ask it for itself and that to be Israel is not to claim it.[28]

So, mythologically or in spiritual fact, Satan has a claim on us. No one is debt-free unless Satan is bought off. 'The Son of Man . . . did not come to be served, but to serve, and to give up his life as a ransom for many.'[29] The ransom model of the atonement, though formally distinct from the satisfaction model, is actually of a piece with it. The satisfaction model requires that God's justice as well as mercy be maintained: there is a debt to God that needs to be paid, not merely waived. To this modernists usually reply that God's loving-kindness is frequently endorsed before the crucifixion and needs no arbitrary payment. Why should God require punitive reprisals against a sinful creation, especially if He intends to pay the price Himself? I do not think the matter is so simple even for those debts we directly owe to God, but the ransom model rebuts modernism anyway. God maintains justice, even for Satan. God Himself will not, and cannot, wholly let us off our debt to the accusers. What He can do is pay it, and thereby satisfy His justice and the devil.

## C Taking metaphors seriously

The formal language I have been using, of debt and satisfaction, must be cashed. It is not enough to say that 'through his wounds we are healed':[30] we do need some acceptable sense in which this might be true, or at least might have some definite, non-sentimental import. Maybe, for some, the verbal music is enough to help them towards an unrevengeful gratitude that will serve our environmental needs. 'Let's think of everything as if it were a gift; forgive our debtors and not be surprised or hurt if they are not so prompt to forgive us.' Maybe our rulers should follow mediaeval practice and make public penance, crawling on their knees, instead of superstitiously relying upon verbal expressions of regret to save their faces. Maybe they would do this better if they held the story of the crucified (or some other saint) within their hearts. But maybe there is more to this than myth. Before saying how, I wish to add a few remarks about the status of metaphorical language. Debt, ransom, satisfaction and the rest are concepts we can grasp in ordinarily human terms, and that provide their own special implications. Debts ought to be paid; ransoms need to be. What the accuser is owed is a debt; what needs to be paid to remove the accuser's influence is a ransom, even if the ransom is only trickery. In one way those we have offended have no claim: it is as true for them as us that 'we might remember not to hate any person, for all are vicious; and not be astonished at any evil, all are deserved'.[31] The most the accuser needs to be offered is a ransom that will be stripped from her at once. But in another way those we have offended do deserve some reparation. Metaphorical language, or language understood as metaphorical, allows a greater complexity of implication, even apparent contradiction, than language understood as literal. The more literal a statement the clearer are its implications; the more metaphorical, the more its implications can be grasped only within a larger web of metaphor. That man is a wolf to man is metaphorical in that it is paired with another aphorism, that men are sheep to the slaughter, and that other implications, as that men are four-footed, are not allowed (though there is no rule about what is or isn't). The language of debt and ransom is not literal: it is not therefore vacuous. Nor does it depend, as I have heard some say, on Thatcherism, monetarism, economic individualism or even money. We acknowledged debts before we invented money, and feared those we took from lest they claim their pay. Indeed, I think it not improbable that the very idea of 'property' took shape as what was owned, and lent us, by the gods, including the spirits of the beasts we hunted and the land we ploughed. What was first theirs, we borrowed in fear, or made up rituals to let us think they had given permission. The notion that human beings could 'own' the land (that is, could dispose of it, or alter it, at will) or their neighbours arrived by slow degrees: priest-kings impersonating gods, or incarnating them, as they discovered in themselves the power to cow and to control. It is not that we first invented private property, and then attributed our notions to the God beyond all gods: the very notion of property came from religion, from our sense of living in a world we still don't control. Our first attempts at payment were propitiation. Our first attempts at speech itself were certainly not literal.

This has wider implications than I shall uncover here. The easy assumption is that the primary context of our speech is literal and unassuming, and that it is only later that we employ familiar phrases in a 'metaphorical' mode, or on stage, or within quotation marks. The 'real' meaning of a phrase is what it is used for in that primary setting, and all other use is (non-pejoratively) deviant. Derrida's infamous dispute with Searle about the proper interpretation of Austin is so laced, to ordinarily analytic eyes, with confusion and innuendo that its merits have been ignored by analysts, and its demerits praised by Derrideans.[32] Derrida's point (or the one of them I choose to follow up) is that Austin assumes too readily that we can identify non-deviant uses as primary, whereas the very possibility of speaking 'straight' requires that we can also quote and parody and speak-in-character. If we could not quote what has been said we could never have said it. If we could not depict a promise upon stage we could not promise. We can go further. On the one hand, the conventions that allow someone to 'speak on stage' without being held to what was said are not universal;[33] on the other, those who promise (not 'on stage') are acting in a kind of play themselves. Once again, we did not first invent, say, marriage and then imagine that the gods got married: marrying is an invocation of Earth and Heaven, or (equivalently) a drama. So, at first, was dramatic art itself.

Intelligible speech, in short, is not first about what we now reckon sensible realities and then about the realms of fiction or the supernatural, as if we first talked about electro-magnetic radiation and only later extended the word to cover spiritual illumination. At first, all forms of sudden clarity are light: what we distinguish as the solar Sun, and the Sun of Righteousness are originally one experience, one story. Accordingly, it is the 'literal' meaning that is slowly carved out of the first, fictional endeavour. What we owe becomes 'literal debt' when we have decided upon simple, final means of payment in a certain range of cases: when, in short, we are agreed on how to buy each other off. Original debts are not so easily defined, nor easily displaced.

The very ideas of literal meaning, and literal truth, are themselves so laced with metaphor as to allow an easy puzzle. If metaphorical utterances were not to be taken seriously, or judged 'really true' we should have to concede that literal utterance could not be true, or serious, either. For we have no informative analysis of what the truth of propositions rests in that is not metaphorical. If 'grass is green' is true upon occasion that is because the expression 'grass is green' mirrors, or represents, or calls to mind the grass's greenness. But all those paraphrases were metaphors. If they weren't really true, then neither is grass green.[34] It follows that the dream of disentangling 'literal' and 'deviant' meaning, 'real' truth and fiction, is no more than a dream (and also no less than a dream). I have often spoken, in this monograph, of spirits, gods and stories, and occasionally paused to remark that these could be taken to be real and causally active entities, or else merely ways of expressing policies, or describing moods. That distinction has its uses, but it is a tool of art and not a simple description of what, obviously, is 'there'. Are gods and planetary spirits fictions? Maybe so, but so are human selves as well. Are human beings real? Of course, but so are human moods, and human dreams.

## D Paying off the debt

So how can we pay off our debt? The first step is to realize we must. Corporeal existence may itself be a fall of sorts, but there is evidence of a closer fall, a degradation and pollution of the world in which we live. Our usual response to those we injure is contempt and fear: we invent good reasons for our injuring them so as not to feel that we have done them wrong or owe them anything. We need to forgive our enemies for the wrongs we did to them before we can face our duty to restore their loss. For much the same reason we need to forgive our benefactors. Before we can make peace with God, with Being as such, we must make peace with them.

> If you are bringing your offering to the altar and there remember that your brother has something against you, leave your offering there before the altar, go and be reconciled with your brother first, and then come back and present your offering. Come to terms with your opponent in good time while you are still on the way to the court with him, or he may hand you over to the judge, and the judge to the officer, and you will be thrown into prison. I tell you solemnly, you will not get out till you have paid the last penny.[35]

I will not rehearse again the reasons for remembering that we injure more than people by our acts, that other creatures have their grievances against us.

The second step is to realize the human impossibility of paying our debt, or satisfying our creditors. Even if those now alive and loving forgave us, there are many dead, and many of the living can do nothing now but endure. Even if we convince ourselves that some of those we injure would forgive us if they could, the fact is that they don't. A dog may fawn upon the mistress that beats him, but does not thereby forgive: nothing the dog can do, any more than a similarly treated child, relieves the debt. Even less can the land forgive us our neglect. The land belongs to God – which is to say, not us – and is owed its sabbaths.[36] No more than animals or hired servants or any without human protectors may the land be exploited wholly for our profit. If we forget that iron rule (as, of course, we have forgotten it), we may justly expect expulsion: 'then indeed the land will rest and observe its sabbaths.'[37] If all those that died untimely or suffered at our hands are raised into that sabbath then there is, maybe, some recompense for them. But even this is not a due return for what they endured, since it is only what God intended for them anyway.

Berry modifies a comment of Orwell's that 'we all live by robbing Asiatic coolies, and those of us who are "enlightened" all maintain that those coolies ought to be set free; but our standard of living, and hence our "enlightenment", demands that the robbery shall continue': *pari passu* 'we all live by robbing nature, but our standard of living demands that the robbery shall continue'.[38] This fact, by the way, should warn us against historical self-righteousness: 'the probability is overwhelming that if we had belonged to the generations we deplore, we too would have behaved deplorably. The probability is high that we *belong* to a generation that will be found by its successors to have behaved deplorably.'[39]

So we owe a debt that we cannot pay (and therefore show no signs of even trying to pay), and from which we cannot be released unless some other undertakes to pay instead. How can the debt be paid, and who shall pay it? One model of payment may be simply that we suffer too, and thereby satisfy the requirement of justice, that none profit by her sin, but rather pay for it. But the pay must include some recompense to those offended, not merely that we suffer as they did. 'Pay' is of course a slightly misleading image: whatever the pay turns out to be it will not retrospectively justify our former sins. We cannot buy the right to oppress or kill: 'Of whom could [we] purchase such a right? Who could make such a conveyance?'[40] But though we cannot justify, we can perhaps set straight, or one can do it for us. What seems to be required is not merely that one suffers alongside the victims, but that they are supported through that time, and brought thereby to greater glories. Only those are fully recompensed who rise with the One victim into life immortal, because they have been coaxed into forgiving the oppressor. But those who, animated by the accuser, only wish to see their oppressors suffer, may accept that satisfaction if no worse calamity could come. They may accept another's suffering in recompense if they can be convinced that it was all that other's fault in the first place.

If there is to be justice in forgiveness then someone must endure all evil inflicted on creation, and offer at once a spectacle of sin revenged, and a hope of life renewed. If there is to be the latter there must be a new world made through that sacrifice; if there is to be the former the sacrifice must be that one through which the old world was made. Who better to provide the accusers with the spectacle they have some right to claim than the one that provided the occasion for the offences that they avenge? Who better to provide new hope than one through whom worlds are made? Thus: some are shaken from their grief and fury by the sight of someone willing to endure beside them, and forgive; some are grimly glad to see the First Offender put to the torment that His act occasioned, and have no more grudge to harbour against lesser crooks. In sum, only one believed to be as God can pay our debts, whether He thereby opens up new worlds where past evil is irrelevant, or acknowledges His responsibility in making the world where evil was done before.

Moltmann perhaps reached similar conclusions: 'If Christ is the ground of salvation for the whole creation, for sinful men and women, and for "enslaved" non-human creatures, he is then also the ground for the existence of the whole creation, human beings and nature alike.'[41] God's self-limiting in creation, whereby he allows the existence of distinct beings, and his self-limiting in redemption, whereby he buys us out of the long cycle, are, in eternity, the very same. I have sought to expound this paradox elsewhere: here the intention is to explore its significance for 'the environment'.

The new heaven and earth that James Watt expected were born in the resurrection from the dead. When we were 'dead in trespasses and sin' we hated those we injured, and those who injured us. We sought to secure ourselves against the coming trials by heaping up more riches, honours, skills (and so did greater injury to those we abused or robbed). We sought to secure ourselves by showing ourselves ready to punish others for their real or imagined sins. When we can believe ourselves forgiven – by God and by our neighbour – we can ourselves forgive. When we see God Himself accepting His responsibility, we can as well. The exemplary model, in its way, is right: at least *our* world is changed by it, the light in which we see things. That the world we see, the light we see it by, is a celestial realm, the one closed off since Eden shut its gates, may say more than a secular psychologist would wish. At the very least the Atonement story makes a change in us, and one that weakens the demands of fear and hatred. Until we believe ourselves forgiven we cannot endure the light, and hurriedly return to building walls against it.

## E Judgement Day

Etymologically, ecology is the study of an *oikos*, a household: call it 'domestic science'.[42] The *oikos* of our concern is the whole earth, as someday it may be a larger world. That earth is the Lord's. This means, at least, that it is not ours, and that, to the attentive eye, it shows itself in glory, lit by the *Shekhinah* who accompanies Israel in their exile, and God's creation in its degradation. 'Creation still retains the hope of being freed, like us, from its slavery to decadence, to enjoy the same freedom and glory as the children of God.'[43] Creation's groans, and ours, may not be put in words, 'but the Spirit himself expresses our plea'. God himself, through the Spirit, is embodied in creation, and there pays us for existing. That there is a real, a 'personal' embodiment is the particular thesis of Christian tradition. Other branches of the Abrahamic tradition have preferred to see God's Word 'embodied', as it were, in the Koran, the Torah or the continuing Israel. All of us, to some extent, have lost the sense that these embodiments include creation, but none can truthfully deny it. Nor can any of us deny that the same Word may be found elsewhere: that is what is meant by saying it is the Word, not a word.

Can we evade the judgement?

> 'Listen to another parable. There was a man, a landowner, who planted a vine-yard; he fenced it round, dug a winepress in it and built a tower; then he leased it to tenants and went abroad. When vintage time drew near he sent his servants to the tenants to collect his produce. But the tenants seized his servants, thrashed one, killed another and stoned a third. Next he sent some more servants, this time a larger number, and they dealt with them in the same way. Finally he sent his son to them. "They will respect my son", he said. But when the tenants saw the son, they said to each other, "This is the heir. Come on, let us kill him and take over his inheritance". So they seized him and threw him out of the vineyard and killed him. Now when the owner of the vineyard comes, what will he do to those tenants?'[44]

Parables, *pace* the editors of the Jerusalem Bible, are not entirely allegories, as if 'the proprietor is God; the vineyard the Chosen People; the servants the prophets; the son Jesus' and so on. God is not really an 'absentee landlord', reaping, as in another parable, what he has not sown. Jesus poses his audience a problem – having to do with a time when unclaimed property could be expected to be available to first comers[45] – in the language of Isaiah, and asked what they would expect, by the standards they had lived by. 'Woe to those who add house to house, and join field to field until everywhere belongs to them and they are the sole inhabitants of the land.'[46] Isaiah's prophecy or observation was that 'Yahweh aflame with anger against his people has raised his hand to strike them. . . . He hoists a signal for a distant nation, he whistles it up from the ends of the earth; and look, it comes, swiftly, promptly.' Jesus' audience doubtless expected much the same climax, the destruction and exile of Israel at the hands of a new people as brutal as the Assyrians. That same people, no doubt, would one day be faced by God's intransigence: 'when the Lord has completed all his work on Mount Zion and in Jerusalem he will punish what comes from the king of Assyria's boastful heart, and his arrogant insolence.'[47] Those who claim the land, and their successes, as their own, who 'rose to suppose themselves kings over all things created',[48] must fear the sword of the divine judgement, dividing this from that.

> The day of Yahweh is coming, merciless, with wrath and fierce anger, to reduce the earth to desert and root out the sinners from it. . . . Babylon, that pearl of kingdoms, the jewel and boast of Chaldaeans, like Sodom and Gomorrah shall be overthrown by God. Never more will anyone live there or be born there from generation to generation. No Arab will pitch his tent there, nor shepherds feed their flocks, but beasts of the desert will lie there, and owls fill its houses. Ostriches will make their homes there and satyrs have their dances there. Hyenas will call to each other in its keeps, jackals in the luxury of its palaces . . . Its time is almost up, its days will not last long.[49]

Or in Berry's words: '[Nature] is plainly saying to us: "if you put the fates of whole communities or cities or regions or ecosystems at risk in single ships or factories or powerplants, then I will furnish the drunk or fool or imbecile who will make the necessary small mistake".'[50] That should be enough.

> There was no need of a steed nor a lance to pursue them;
> it was decreed their own deed, and not chance, should undo them.[51]

At the far side of tribulation, God will restore the land, Isaiah said.

> Once more there will be poured on us the spirit from above; then shall the wilderness be fertile land and fertile land become forest. In the wilderness justice will come to live and integrity in the fertile land. . . . My people will live in a

peaceful home, in safe houses, in quiet dwellings. . . . Happy will you be, sowing by every stream, letting ox and donkey roam free.[52]

God will restore the land for those who will obey his laws (to allow all things their place): 'the redeemed will walk there, for those Yahweh has ransomed shall return.' Until that time we may, gloomily, suspect that peoples will rise and fall, the desert expand and brambles grow till they are cut back by fire. We may, yet more gloomily, suspect that the little cycles of slash-and-burn agriculture and exploitation now encompass the whole globe, that there may be an environmental crisis from which we won't recover to be struck down again. If we forget our danger, or brood on it as inescapable and final, we shall be lost. If we can believe that there is a better way, on the far side of imaginable disaster, maybe we shall, beyond all reasonable hope, discomfort Jonah.[53]

## Notes

1.  E. Muir, *Collected Poems* (Faber: London, 1960) p. 200.

2.  M. Fox, *Creation Spirituality* (Harper: San Francisco, 1991), pp. 1f.

3.  Michael Howard, Secretary of State for the Environment, to the RSPB/Green Alliance Conference, 30 October 1992. Quite what 'sustainable development' actually means in practice is another question.

4.  T. Jefferson, *Writings* V, p. 116; cited in S. G. Brown, *The First Republicans* (Syracuse University Press: Syracuse, NY, 1954), p. 12.

5.  Leviticus 25.23 (JB); see J. Hart, *The Spirit of the Earth* (Paulist Press: New Jersey, 1984), pp. 69f. One American tragedy is that incomers refused to see that Native Americans and incomers could share a vision.

6.  Al-Hafiz B. A. Mazri, 'Islam and ecology', p. 7 in F. Khalid and J. O'Brien (eds), *Islam and Ecology* (Cassell: London and New York, 1992), pp. 1–23.

7.  O. Llewellyn, 'Desert reclamation and conservation in Islamic law', p. 89, in Khalid and O'Brien, *Islam and Ecology*, pp. 87–97.

8.  Empedocles, fr. 130, in G. Kirk, J. E. Raven and M. Schofield (eds), *The Presocratic Philosophers* (Cambridge University Press: Cambridge, 1983), p. 318, § 412 (reading 'men' for 'people' without warrant in the Greek).

9.  Empedocles, fr. 115, ibid., p. 315, § 401.

10.  Empedocles, ibid., p. 317, § 410.

11.  See M. Palmer, 'The Protestant tradition', p. 95, in E. Breuilly and M. Palmer

(eds), *Christianity and Ecology* (Cassell: London and New York, 1992), pp. 86–97.

12. Quoted by C. Hollis, *The Mind of Chesterton* (Hollis & Carter: London, 1970), p. 69.

13. G. K. Chesterton, *Orthodoxy* (Fontana: London, 1961; first published 1908), p. 66; see my *God's World and the Great Awakening*, op. cit., pp. 40f.

14. G. M. Hopkins, 'God's Grandeur' in *Poems of Gerard Manley Hopkins*, ed. W. H. Gardner and N. H. Mackenzie (Oxford University Press: London, 1970), p. 66.

15. Muir, 'The Transfiguration' in *Collected Poems*, p. 199.

16. Fox, *Creation Spirituality*, p. 19; he does later speak of justice: ibid., p. 25.

17. J. M. Soskice, 'Creation and religion', p. 44 in R. Williams (ed.), *Creation, Christians and the Environment* (Newman Association Papers 1990), pp. 36–45.

18. S. Heine, *Christianity and the Goddesses*, tr. J. Bowker (SCM: London, 1988), p. 46.

19. See my *Civil Peace and Sacred Order* (Clarendon Press: Oxford, 1989), p. 172.

20. R. Jeffers, *The Double Axe and Other Poems* (Liveright: New York, 1977), pp. 47f.

21. My *The Mysteries of Religion* (Blackwell: Oxford, 1986), p. 240: 'the Aztec empire, one may suspect, was toppled so easily because its ruling people could no longer endure the headless corpse that wandered their hallucinatory forest, the hideous wound in its chest opening and closing with the sound of a woodman's axe.'

22. J. Glenn Gray, *The Warriors: Reflections on Men in Battle* (Harper & Row: New York, 1970; 1st edn 1959), p. 203; see Jeffers, *Double Axe*, pp. 145f.

23. Matthew 18.23ff.

24. R. Dumont, cited by S. George, *How the Other Half Dies* (Penguin: Harmondsworth, 1976), p. 53.

25. Ecclesiasticus 28.2ff. (JB).

26. Fox, *Creation Spirituality*, p. 119.

27. Mishna, tractate Yoba, pp. 852–85b; cited by E. Levinas, *Nine Talmudic Readings*, tr. A. Aronowicz (Indiana University Press: Bloomington and Indianapolis, 1990), p. 12.

28. Levinas, *Nine Talmudic Readings*, p. 29.

29. Matthew 20.28 (NEB).

30. 1 Peter 2.24, after Isaiah 53.5.

31. Jeffers, *Double Axe*, pp. 145f.

32. J. Derrida, 'Signature event context', *Glyph* 1 (1977), pp. 172–97; J. Searle,

'Reiterating the differences', *Glyph* 1 (1977), pp. 198–208; J. Derrida, 'Limited Inc abc', *Glyph* 2 (1977), pp. 162–354.

33. Which is why it is insufficient, under Islamic rules, to say that Rushdie only 'quoted' or 'represented' the offending words, without himself 'endorsing' them. That is not to say that the death sentence is just, though it does not rest upon the word of one 'mad mullah', as the British press supposes.

34. See my 'The truth of metaphor', *International Journal of Philosophical Studies* (1994) (forthcoming).

35. Matthew 5.23ff. (JB).

36. Leviticus 25.23; see Deuteronomy 24.14ff.

37. Leviticus 26.34 (JB).

38. Berry, *What Are People For?* (Rider Books: London, 1990), p. 201.

39. Berry, ibid. p. 81.

40. J. Lawrence, *A Philosophical Treatise on Horses and The Moral Duties of Man towards the Brute Creation* (1796: 2nd edn 1802, 3rd edn 1810); excerpted in E. B. Nicholson, *The Rights of an Animal* (Kegan Paul: London, 1879), p. 92.

41. J. Moltmann, *God in Creation*, tr. M. Kohl (SCM: London, 1985), p. 94.

42. G. Paris, *Pagan Meditations*, tr. G. Moore (Spring Publications: Dallas, 1986), p. 176.

43. Romans 8.21ff. (JB).

44. Matthew 21.33ff. (JB).

45. See J. Jeremias, *The Parables of Jesus*, tr. S. H. Hooke (SCM Press: London, 1973), third edn), pp. 70ff.: the tenants presumably thought that the builder must be dead.

46. Isaiah 5.8 (JB).

47. Isaiah 10.12 (JB).

48. R. Kipling, *Verse 1885–1926* (Hodder & Stoughton: London, 1927), p. 313.

49. Isaiah 13.9, 19–22 (JB).

50. Berry, *What Are People For?*, p. 203.

51. Kipling, *Verse*, p. 314.

52. Isaiah 32. 15–20 (JB).

53. It is noteworthy that the one biblical prophet to have clearly succeeded in reforming anyone is the one most obviously a fiction!

# Conclusions

## A Global religions

In a brief study presented to the Society of Christian Philosophers some years ago[1] I distinguished various kinds of 'religion' or 'morale' that might unite our struggling millions in a global order. Even a global empire would need some unifying, supportive factor of this kind. But it is chiefly, in Hocking's words, 'because we do not want a world state, [that] we do require a world morale'.[2] The kind that universalists like Kant have hoped for is one that any rational person must agree to: 'There can be only one religion which is valid for all men and at all times. Thus the different confessions can scarcely be more than the vehicles of religion.'[3] Others have suspected that the single boat in which we shall, perhaps, all sail will have been patched together from a thousand swarming vessels, that its unity will be eclectic rather than systematic. Others again have hoped that it will be their religion that is the sole survivor: neither eclectic nor demonstrable from any set of rational axioms, but simply, so they tell us, true.

Good liberal secularists, of course, may say that they can do without religion. Religious forms are divisive in their nature, and any overarching, global order must decree that no one sect gain greater power than others, that decisions be taken by non-sectarian principles. The trouble is that all attempts to state those principles reveal quite quickly how sectarian the liberals are. All the great religions, we are regularly and misleadingly informed, speak of the Fatherhood of God and the Brotherhood of Man (or else they aren't great religions) – notions that good liberals have divested of their supernaturalist ring. It is axiomatic that Hindu respect for cows, for example, is a superstition or a personal life-choice, and humanist respect for people is an obvious, rational law. It is axiomatic that the *Shari'a*, the law of Islam, is inferior to, and must be subject to the United Nations Declaration on Human Rights. Obviously, we ought to support needy strangers, and just as obviously we need not support our unborn children. Obviously people ought to learn to move about, without a settled homeland and without more than romantic memories of their ancestral angels. The powerful are at their most doctrinaire and moralistic when they think they are being 'impartial'. Liberal secularists, in fact, rarely have good arguments to prove that their particular intuitions are much more than echoes of an older, Kantian moralism. Like most other rulers of empires they do sincerely think that their own customs are obviously superior to all others. The others may disagree, but are at present forced to admit that liberal, or illiberal, secularists are helped by the technical and economic dominance of Western countries. 'Liberal or illiberal': some secularists are liberal, and really believe that individual people should be helped to share in the wealth and wisdom made by humankind, without being positively *made* to abandon their old customs (except when they are really wrong). Other secularists are illiberal, and sincerely believe that almost everything that has been said or done before the 'scientific era' is worth nothing. People, being self-domesticated primates, need the guidance of eugenicists, who will permit (or help) the destruction of defective types in the name of a 'peaceful' future. It seems not to trouble such illiberal theorists much that every ruler who has tried to do this openly is now regarded with contempt and fear.

Both liberal and illiberal Western universalists have a religion: both carry an image of what humankind should be, and how the world should be explained; both have their heroes, and their sacred texts and clerisies. Both may struggle to accommodate the notion of environmental risk: liberals may acknowledge that the needs of future (human) generations, both technical and aesthetic, require some self-restraint on people now. Illiberals may prefer to use things up in the hope that (by so doing) they'll create the basis for a superrace: why trouble about the feeble satisfactions of the half-men if there is a chance of making supermen?

There are other options for a world-morale, and ones that I would reckon safer. But these too are often very different from each other, and acknowledge no common authority. The eclectic solution is to mix and match existing cults, on condition that all cultists pay their due respect to the world-empire: just so King Belshazzar gathered the sacred vessels from the conquered nations, 'drank wine and praised their gods of gold and silver, of bronze and iron, of wood and stone'[4] (very much as moderns praise the artistry of mediaeval cathedrals, icons, ancient statues). Maybe liberals will settle for this, since religion cannot yet be wished away: what matters is our cultural roots, our humane and artistic sensibility, and every marvellous god can be admired as long as no one is so bad-mannered as to denounce another. Maybe this is already a world religion, and may at least allow a little force to local shrines and customs. But it does not seem so insistently eclectic as to forbid commercial exploitation where the rulers want it: after all, aesthetic or ethnic feelings must give way before the real god, of money, or progress, or the rulers' whim. And most of the cults it borrows from will be resistant. Christians may see the beast of Revelation mouthing 'bombast and blasphemy' with the support of its marvel-working companion. Buddhists may see a willed entanglement in the nets of death and illusion. Muslims will detect the *Dar al-Harb*, with which there can be no lasting truce.

Whereas universalists believe that there is only one way reason can accept, and eclecticists require us to 'believe' – but not to believe *true* – whatever anyone at all believes, faith-holders of whatever faith insist upon particular beliefs from many possible, and possibly rational, ones. Particular historical faiths can simply be identified, compared and judged by whatever standard judges find to use. It may be slightly more helpful to classify them as follows.

Some projected world religions accept a division between spiritual authority and power and some do not. On the one side: Hinduism draws a distinction between Brahmin and Kshatriya; Gautama chose to be a Buddha, not a Cakravartin (a world-ruler); Christians, Jews and Muslims all find their authorities elsewhere than in princes. On the other side, the half-forgotten but still deeply influential experiments of Egyptian Pharaonism, Constantinian theocracy, the Imamate, Tibetan Buddhism (under one interpretation) all postulate a God-King present in the flesh.

Again, some presuppose a diffused authority, others a more central one: for some any believer may speak God's words; for others only accredited officials may. Some admit their status as faith-holders; others claim to be uniquely rational, so that mere exposition should convince (and those who aren't convinced are knaves). Some believe in progress and reject all sacred limits upon human action (of which the chief example is 'industrialism', or what I called illiberal secularism); others doubt that we can climb to heaven. Some are strongly humanist, others 'naturist'; some are linear in temporal outlook (even if not progressivist), others cyclical; some are Platonic, or supernaturalist, and others not; some rationalist and others mystical; some are tied to particular historical associations, others are relatively abstractable.

## B World Pharaoh

Of all these options four stand out, from somewhat different perspectives: Pharaonism, secularized Buddhism, polytheistic naturism, and sacramental theism. A Pharaonic, naturist, progressivism might suit GEA well, though I suspect not Gaia. Such a credo might too easily excuse industrial excesses, as well as markedly illiberal politics. The dreadful shambles of the Soviet experiment should warn us that collectivist solutions, run by élites, have not done well of late. Maybe the Incas and the Egyptians managed, but their world was narrower. Maybe there is a case for the caste structure which would likely follow in the wake of Pharaoh. People would be tied, by descent and training, to particular lands or crafts, that would all feel, or hope to feel, like organs of a greater Self. Maybe a few would be allowed the illusion of an individual freedom, cloistered within academies to speculate, without direct effect on anything outside. As Belloc remarked,

> If this modern capitalist England could, by a process sufficiently slow to allow for the readjustment of individual interests, be transformed into a Collectivist State, the apparent change at the end of the transition would not be conspicuous to the most of us, and the transition itself should have met with no shocks that theory can discover.[5]

Those of us who favour individualist societies, places where all responsible adults can get on with their individual lives even if they also have some duties, to their children, nation and historic ruler, are often very suspicious of environmentalists because we see them as collectivists. Those of us who are concerned about the cumulative effect of many individual decisions on the land we need are often very suspicious of individualists because we see them as dangerous egotists. On the one hand, the impulse to demand collective action, directed by some one authority ('somebody', we say of every social evil, 'should do something'); on the other, the impulse to resist conscription, to demand that each of us be ruled by our own will, and be no one's slave.

> Howso' great their clamour, whatsoe'er their claim,
> Suffer not the old King under any name!
> *Here is naught unproven – here is naught to learn.*
> *It is written what shall fall if the King return.*
> He shall mark our goings, question whence we came,
> Set his guards about us, as in Freedom's name. . . .
> *All the right they promise – all the wrong they bring,*
> *Stewards of the Judgment, suffer not this King!*[6]

But merely by quoting Kipling, I have given notice that the alternative to despotism is not lawlessness. Despotism *is* lawlessness. 'This is the State above the Law. The State exists for the State alone.'[7] The law by which free peoples live includes requirements of mercy and responsibility that outlaw egotists and fantasists alike. Collectivism – the thesis that the group (or its leader) will manage the land and all its denizens for the good of all (as its leader pretends to see it) – may succeed if the leader really does believe herself a god, or the child of god, who must be worthy of her nature and her ancestry. But that is just to say that collectivism may work if the individual who *does* control things is 'responsible'. If there is no law to which the ruler bows, if Caesar's word *is* law, then we have no reason to expect fair play. Better, as Jefferson required, to suppose that 'it is by dividing and subdividing these republics from the great National one down thr' all its subordinations, until it ends in the administration of every man's farm and affairs by himself [and all under law] that all will be done for the best'.[8] Better still, allow the same prerogative to every creature, and the chance to form alliances. Better dismantle or distribute power, than increase or centralize it.

## C The 'Buddhist' option

The second major option for a world morale may emerge from Buddhist sources. At present the chief influence from that tradition upon environmentalists is via Schumacher's notion of 'Buddhist economics', or Sahlins' 'Zen solution' to the problem of scarcity.[9] This is simply to suggest that we should not be tempted by excessive pleasures, expansive or progressive policies, but identify what we can actually find without imposing burdens on the land and on our neighbours, and adapt our wishes to what we can get. This is to endorse the ancient disdain for *pleonexia*, and to promote what might, in our own history, be far more fitly called the Cynic, or Epicurean, or Christian answers. The problem is that only the committed sage, and the enduring poor, can really expect to practise this. Hunter-gatherers, Sahlins suggests, live in subjective luxury (or did until we began to take their lands away). They know where they can find the things they want, and have no need, or incentive, to accumulate. Such peoples are egalitarian (without the curse of class-division) and, subjectively, well off. Agrarian and industrial societies create a class of owners even as they allow accumulation, and create the hope or expectation that our prospects will improve. When only 'the rich' could ever hope to live at more than 'subsistence level', the damage we did was less (though still significant). Now that we encourage everyone (however unrealistically) to aim for a life requiring massive waste of energy and time and matter, it is remarkably optimistic to suppose that the bills are payable. We are borrowing upon our future expectations of an increased yield, rather than tailoring our demands to what can rationally be expected.

But those who restrain their desires do so because their desires are weak enough to be restrained.[10] There is no reason to believe that the rich will greatly reduce their impact on the world, even if they change their noisier habits; how can the poor be asked to do so, even before they have the impact? We are not hunter-gatherers, and very few of us will ever seek to imitate them (as the Cynics, partly, did). Diogenes, it is said, first kept a cloak, a satchel and a cup, but seeing a boy drink water from his hand, abandoned the cup as well. We won't. We hardly even believe we should, because we recognize that others get their livelihood by selling, painting and making cups, by digging clay and making potters' wheels. We are regularly told to spend, in order to get the wheels of commerce turning. Spending without restraint, of course, on things we do not want except to sell is bound to lead to personal, national and eventually global disaster. Facilitating the exchange of genuine goods is good; merchandising, playing the middle-man (so that one buys to sell) is dangerous; usury, the multiplication of mere money through the enslavement of the debtor, is forbidden in the strongest terms by most of the great religions. They did not succeed in suppressing it, but perhaps controlled it: 'Like every body of moral and religious doctrines, Islam can do no more than, at best, limit, among a certain number of the rich and powerful, the tendency to abuse the power and wealth they possess.'[11]

The rich will not restrain themselves, and laws against industrialist inflation will not succeed – unless, after all, there is a massive shift of feeling. Different Buddhist traditions can be as different as are Rabbinic Judaism, Protestantism, Catholicism, Orthodoxy, Sunni Islam, Shi'a (the major members of what I have labelled Abrahamism), but they all reject Identity. It is a theme that has had an unexpected echo in modern Western thought. Findlay, describing the Wittgensteinian revolution, declared that there was 'no sense of "same" which corresponds more closely with the nature of things than any other', and that this was – by implication – a *welcome* 'charter of freedom'.[12] There is no one abiding thing that is 'the same' throughout the stretch from Stephen's conception (early 1945) till Stephen's death (sometime). We can apply a word to all of it (say, 'Stephen') as we can to the stretch from mitochondrial Eve (the putative ancestress of all living hominids) to humankind's extinction (say, 'humankind'). Our language may encourage each of us here-now to identify more closely with a particular past or future thing, but this does not (on such a theory) represent a clearer or more cogent truth than any other commitment. On this account it matters much less than we think who it is that gets the pleasure that we currently desire. A sufficiently secular Buddhism begins to look like Global Utilitarianism, with the advantage that it can offer meditation exercises to convince us, deeply, of our non-existence, and so enable us to act as global utilitarians should. The only reason that the Organ Lottery[13] would not be adopted as a sane idea in such a world is that no one would want to be saved by such a transplant.

A sufficiently secular Buddhism might make us ready to accept the global calculations. But the perils of global utilitarianism are well-known, and the way in which all real moral decisions are made behind the scenes, most probably by the ruler's clerks. Such a morale, once more, may serve GEA, by reconciling enough of us to dreadful choices, but is as likely to excite revolt – even by those same Buddhists whose ideas are pillaged. For abandoning Identity was not a device for serving global utility (as if 'pleasure' was the key), but for revealing what our egos hide: which is, the Unborn and Indestructible. Though Buddhists regularly, and rightly, deny that we should be loyal to any 'gods', those gods are the fallen or fragmentary images that Abrahamic theists also reject.

> The Buddhist's declaration of her faith, in her enlightened Lord, in the Doctrine or Law of Righteousness he preached, and in the community of those who have 'entered the stream', is not merely a formal analogy to the Christian confession. It defines the particular spiritual route through danger that Buddhists take. . . . Similarly Christians put their faith in the Father, in Jesus, in the Spirit that must animate the fellowship of all believers.[14]

Buddhists and Abrahamists are united in being disengaged from 'the gods of the heathen', but can also recognize that those same gods express a truth.

> Even if we retain any sense of a divine presence in the world, we have to admit that it manifests itself in innumerably various, apparently clashing and conflicting, often inscrutably odd and terrifying ways. Divine unity, not divine plurality, requires an effort of reflection and faith to attain it; and when attained, it does not necessarily exclude plurality.[15]

In brief, we may believe that truth is 'one, without a flaw', and that there is a Beauty that contains all beauties, but that Beauty is Infinite and Indescribable. Any picture we have of how the world should be is bound to be imperfect, incomplete and fragmentary. Even polytheists (whether naturist or Hindu) can recall the God beyond all gods, while still insisting that we pay our dues to local deities and partial views. The moral would seem to be: 'think globally; act locally'. Or – in the context of a 'Buddhistic' global religion – combine the view of ourselves as fragments, defined by the words we choose to use, with respect for those same fragments. Even if nothing in 'fact' says that we are individuals, we must pretend to be. We certainly gain nothing for the whole by dropping that pretence (or by pretending to).

## D Goddesses of stream and spinney

Some strands of our existing faiths are naturist, some humanist. But 'naturism' as a distinct faith can be distinguished from all other 'great religions', even though it has not yet found its prophet. An early version of twentieth-century naturism mixed nationalism and inhumanism to dreadful effect (with the eager assistance of many fashionable thinkers), but there may yet be better versions. Naturists of this sort empathize with Gaia, and with the little places that can be loved and known by careful attention and controlled imagination. 'Science' is at once admired (as showing us how many are the connections between this and that, how beautiful the overarching order) and distrusted. It must be distrusted because its conclusions are couched in abstract, general and 'objective' terms (far distant from the immediate experience of life-in-earth, and characteristic of the 'masculine' intellect). It must be distrusted because it has been devised to concentrate attention on a world stripped of all value, all significance. Although great scientists actually rely upon their sense of beauty, they are trained to deny all beauty, all significance to the world they uncover, so making it available for our industrial use. 'We do not look at trees either as Dryads or as beautiful objects while we cut them into beams. . . . From this point of view the conquest of Nature appears in a new light. We reduce things to mere Nature *in order that* we may conquer them.'[16]

To bring 'the great Mother' back to life is no great magic. Simply by allowing ourselves to acknowledge the memories and stories we repose in the landscape where we live, we are confronted by a world awash with humanly significant life. The maple tree outside is no mere plant, to be dug up or damaged at our whim. It is the tree that blesses us with blossom (and with sticky seeds), that our children and the cats climbed on, that was here before us and (we hope) hereafter. When we carve the landscape to make roads, fields, factories and houses we must do so with a proper respect for 'local gods', and for the local creatures who serve and embody them. Ecofeminists have cause to think that this approach is feminist in effect: it has so often been women who are left behind to care for their locale while men go off to war or city-work, and has been women who are allowed (or even, to their cost, encouraged) to remember 'old wives' tales' that have not been elevated to the rank of 'scientific truth'. It is by now a truism in developmental circles that it is better to involve the women of an agrarian society in discussions about how to live in the land: it is they who may remember how, and they who will put the new advice into practice.

Such a religion, being localized, contains no single pantheon (apart from Gaia). Even the single sun has many different faces, and even 'seed-time and harvest' do not mean the same in every land and era. Even the non-humans with whom we share our houses aren't the same: cows, horses, dogs, cats, pigs can mean as different things as the very sounds we call them by. They are the vocabulary, so to speak, with which we tell our stories – although this is to forget that they have a voice as well. They share the telling with us.

Can such localized religion serve a global end? I believe it can, as well as nationalism does. 'Nationalism' is not the belief that 'my nation' is the best and brightest, destined to destroy or convert all others: that is better known as imperialism, and is present (in a quieter form) in liberal universalism, blind to all values unfamiliar to its advocates. Nationalism is rather the belief I attributed to Jefferson: that things are best managed when they are managed by the people closest to the problem. Nations need not be exclusive: we can regard ourselves as Northern English, British, even European. Nor need they insist on rigid boundaries. Birds, for whom the ethological use of 'territory' was first established, may sometimes defend a well-defined continuous volume. Mammals rarely do: their territories are paths, that intersect. It is time we remembered this, and then recalled that the 'same landmark' may have as many different meanings as the sun, remembered in the stories of assorted tribes, housed and unhoused. Different peoples see quite different goddesses in 'the same spinney', and can honour the spinney differently. Of course, through long association they may come to think the goddesses are really one: that is, the stories blend together till there is one people.

Has such a religion, multiform and metaphorical, a sacred text? No single text, as yet, but many rural or romantic poets can contribute lines (including, of course, Kipling). The trouble is, as so often, that there may be at least two strands within this faith: the romantic and the inhumanist. Romantics delight in beauty, and in empathetic sorrow for the grave ills of the world; inhumanists, more coldly, see the Way Things Are (or would be if we did not 'interfere') as paramount, and sneer a little at the softness of those who live in houses, close to hospitals. Since first we began to cultivate the land, and tame the animals we shared it with, we have had to reckon on breeding things, and killing them. A rigorous inhumanism must have learned that lesson. What reason is there not to breed our conspecifics, where we have the power? What reason not to look aside from individual people to the line they leave? Once again, there is no sense of 'same' that is more true than others. Such naturists do often adopt an anti-realist posture, partly in revulsion at dogmatic claims to know a 'real truth' that disallows all ordinarily human claims. But if those claims are 'true' that 'we' now seriously endorse, then we can once more define whole tribes as vermin, or insist that there is no single, important individual that corresponds to older, humane notions of an individual. If liberal morality is only what the ruling, masculine classes have gradually devised to save their faces, and 'we' (whoever we now are) are free to devise our own, what stops us devising dreadfully illiberal ones?

In short, and recalling earlier discussions, polytheistic naturists may be as dangerous to humane value as are Pharaonists or selfless utilitarians. All three of them may look like what we need; all three are as open to abuse (what we now call abuse) as is the older way to which I turn.

## E  Sacramental theism

You will recall Toynbee's judgement that 'a right religion is one that teaches respect for the dignity and sanctity of all nature. The wrong religion is one that licenses the indulgence of human greed at the expense of non-human nature.'[17] I am sure that he was right. Right religion, true piety, requires that 'all beings, not only our friends but also our enemies, not only men but also animals and the inanimate, be met with reverence, for all are friends in the friendship of the one to whom we are reconciled in faith.'[18] But it is for that very reason that Toynbee was wrong to say that 'the religion we need to embrace is pantheism, and that the religion we now need to discard is Judaic monotheism and the post-Christian non-theistic faith in scientific progress'. He was wrong, both because he simultaneously conflated and distinguished two 'religions' (monotheism and atheistic, scientific humanism), and because he wrongly imagined that there is Jewish or Christian backing for a belief that 'mankind is morally entitled to exploit the rest of the universe for the indulgence of human greed'. Toynbee's mistake was understandable. Christian missionaries who have taken credit for liberal humanism, scientific progress, industrial expansion, secularism and the city, can hardly complain if a later generation, more conscious of their attendant evils, should blame Christian (or Abrahamic) monotheism for our crisis. But even if responsibility did lie where such missionaries said it does not follow that the attendant evils would have been avoided, or can be cured, by simple reversal of Abrahamic doctrine.

Modern science perhaps did have its beginning in the realization that, since God was not identical with the world, the world was not self-explanatory, need not be the way, as it happens, it is.

> There has always existed at every period an incongruous and perverse class of professors who expounded with equal zeal and confidence both these doctrines at the same time: that we can know everything and that we can know nothing. The latter group says that truth lies hidden in a well, that we know one thing only, namely that we know nothing; and utters a hundred idle paradoxes of the same character, with the hope of acquiring a reputation for profundity. The former party, on the other hand, maintain with remarkable daring that the principles of the Universe can be deduced from the principles of thought, in spite of the fact that these refer only to us. They proclaim, with unaccountable disregard for the truth, that there is nothing which is not open to their understanding.[19]

Herbert was no doubt right to insist, against imbeciles and sceptics, that 'Truth exists, . . . is as eternal or as ancient as things themselves . . . , is everywhere . . . [and] reveals itself'.[20] But we cannot expect to work out scientific truths by thought alone. It is one of the many oddities of modern atheistic science that people who would laugh at the ontological argument now suggest that the world's existence is guaranteed by abstract mathematical principle (and therefore, luckily, needs no further explanation). Herbert, though a Rationalist philosopher, had greater sense. The oddity of past atheistic science has been that scientists have supposed that God's will, being inscrutable, can play no part at all in understanding, that science can be entirely divorced from ethics. The conclusion has been disastrous, but we shall not avoid it by insisting that there is, after all, no distinction between God and the world, that the world is entirely and unambiguously worshipful and *causa sui*.

Liberal humanism perhaps received its strongest, most entrenched support from those who insisted that there are real individuals, immortal souls accountable to God for what they are and do, and that all of humankind is of one kind (at a time when fashionable scientists were suspecting that it wasn't[21]). The catch has been that some have concluded to a rampant egoism and speciesism together. This conclusion too has been disastrous, but it is no solution to insist that after all the individuals there are are *only* segments of a greater whole, or that they 'exist' because our language says they do.

Industrial expansion may have received its start from two convictions found in monotheistic tradition in the West: on the one hand, that those in misery have claims on their neighbours for assistance; on the other, that neither star-demons nor customary practices can stand against the love of God. The catch has been that some have concluded that we are entitled to do anything at all that promises some minor alleviation of distress for human beings. We have imagined that all limits are transcendable, and that all the world is ours. The effect remains in many who *say* that they are against (for example) the capture and slow death of chimpanzees, or the destruction of wetlands, but add that 'obviously people come first': this is simply to license anything that can be made to seem 'humanitarian'. If environmentalism, or 'the liberation of life', is to mean anything we must abandon that consoling lie, that we can have the profits and not bear the guilt. That is why utilitarianism, in all its shifting forms, is another wholly mistaken move: utilitarianism is the denial of debt, and guilt. But it is no answer to these errors to invoke the multitudinous gods of nature, treat AIDS as divine vengeance not to be resisted, and compress our weaker neighbours back into the slots from which a few of us have briefly escaped.

The piety we need to practise, and that a sufficient number all across the globe can practise, is no new one. It must include some recognition of necessity, that we cannot have nor are entitled to whatever advantages we please. It is one thing to agree that we have a duty to protect and care for the poor and defenceless: quite another to pretend that there is an absolute duty to 'improve the world'. Those impulses will prove destructive. As Chesterton said: 'Nobody could pretend that the affectionate mother of a rather backward child *deserves* to be punished by having all the happiness taken out of her life. But anybody can pretend that the act is needed for the happiness of the community.'[22] The only feasible improvements must be to help each other be glad about the world we have, or sometimes to be glad despite the world we have, the world that does not belong to us.

> I tell you naught for your comfort,
> Yea, naught for your desire,
> Save that the sky grows darker yet
> And the sea rises higher.[23]

We may have no success within the circles of this world, and if the world falls to pieces around us we can hardly complain. All that can reasonably sustain us amid triumph or disaster is the conviction that 'our God has blessed creation, calling it good';[24] that there is an eternal, teasing possibility of convivial relationships, mirrored and distorted in this fallen world; that our debts can be paid; that the fate of all is in the hands of each. According to a Talmudic story:

> In a boat at sea, someone began to bore a hole in the bottom of the boat. On being remonstrated with he answered 'I am only boring under my own seat'. 'Yes', said his comrades, 'but when the sea rushes in we shall be drowned with you'. So it is with Israel. Its weal or woe is in the hands of every individual Israelite.

Sacramental theism declares that we do not own the world, but only enjoy its fruits on the condition that we leave as good for others. It declares that Beauty and Justice are not different at different times and places, although their detailed manifestations may (or even must) be, and that there is a true description of the world and of its denizens which denies us any right to redescribe our victims and our sins. The world exists as incarnating Beauty: a beauty that for us is best, most safely, seen in a life responsive to its neighbours and delighting in their beauty. Rabbinic Judaism, Islam and Christianity can all agree that there is one God, one source of life and light. They can even agree that there is one true religion, which is to do justice and love mercy and walk humbly with that God. Believing this, we can also believe that

> you never enjoy the world aright, till the Sea itself floweth in your veins, till you are clothed with the heavens, and crowned with the stars; and perceive yourself to be the sole heir of the whole world, and more than so because men are in it who are every one sole heirs as well as you.[25]

Traherne's error, and others', was to forget that there are others in the world than men, that it is not for 'us' only – unless by 'men' we mean, with Blake, all finite beings everywhere. All those who draw their piety from the Abrahamic line, and many who reach out to justice elsewhere in the world, can acknowledge God, and incarnate Beauty, and the Spirit that groans with us. What is here-now is not entirely beauty, and the world is filled with more than ideal types. Beauty is incarnate – whether in a Galilean *hasid*, or in the people of Israel, or in the Torah or Koran, or anywhere that, for a moment, someone sees the uncreated light. No one who attends to our, and everyone's, double contingency and splendour can then calmly reckon things 'fair game', made solely for our pleasure. We receive all things as gift: if we intercept and deny the gift to others we should not expect to keep it.

Abrahamic believers can see Beauty, however fragmented and distorted, in the world of our experience, and live in hope of being united with true, supernatural beauty. The same is true of Hindus, and of many Buddhist sects. Things as they are contain the seeds or fragments of divinity: we see those seeds and love them. Equal and opposite errors are to imagine that things as they are contain all beauty, and that they are so far distorted as to be no more than caricature or parody of the truth. From those errors the gods, the Buddha-nature, the divine attempt to save us by occasionally presenting themselves in clearer and more compelling ways. The Buddha-nature was visible in other lives than Gautama's, other lives than the merely human. Vishnu the Preserver can take shape as Rama (whose birthplace, at Ayodhya, has recently served as a reminder of the perils of religion), but also as boar, or fish, or stunted child. True religion and undefiled, across the globe, is a response to a divine challenge: to live as children of the gods. The universe, as Marcus Aurelius said, is in love with creating: so I will love too. What we create here-now will always be no more than fragment. We can neither identify it wholly with the gods, nor conceive it in the absence of the gods. To be at all is to be Something, and that Thing, imperfectly represented as it may be, is an aspect of the Divine Life, seen aright only when we see it in the context of that life. 'These gods are visions of the eternal attributes, or divine names, which, when erected into gods, become destructive of humanity. . . . When separated from man or humanity, who is Jesus the Saviour, the vine of eternity, they are thieves and rebels, they are destroyers.'[26] 'Humanity', remember, does not mean 'the worm of seventy winters', but the embodied Word of God.

It is risky to claim that 'every religion' says much the same. There are undoubtedly manifold divergences and disagreements, even to the death, and it is obvious enough that every attempt to state points of agreement, as if they were the essence of religion, turns out to be a feebler version of the speaker's own ancestral creed. Kant, Vedantin mystics, naturists and sacramental theists (like myself) who claim to have seen into the 'real meaning' and the unity of creeds that others think diverse deserve some scorn. It is often right to attend to differences, not similarities. My only excuse must be that we are now in need of something that can engage us all. We need a vision that will help us through the years: pantheism will not do, nor technophiliac obsession of the kind that dismisses all past happenings as out-of-date. It follows that some environmentalist rhetoric, though well-intentioned, is dangerous. Any merely sectarian, abusive response to the danger that we face gets nowhere. Attempts to speak the language of the time (progress, development, stewardship) result in schemes that actually exacerbate our problem. Better that we think of ourselves as children of earth and starry heaven than that we commit ourselves to one parent only. Better that we see incarnate beauties as real fragments of the god we can only gesture at. Better that we find some way of acknowledging our guilt without being poisoned by it. Better that we seek to draw the world of our experience into the world of imagination, than that we limit our imagination to what is here and now, or turn aside entirely to imagined worlds.

I began this book by comparing us all to alcoholics, who need to be awakened to a real assent, and a better life. Addicts are not well served by speaking only of the evils of their plight, nor by abusing – however justly – their intelligence and self-control. Even if they can forbear they will still wish for what they must not have, and never wholly cure themselves. That may be our condition. If there is any deeper and more lasting hope it must come by finding the convivial world, the world 'where Jesus is at home', a real presence and continuing inspiration. We have been sustained in recent years by the conviction that things will always be getting better: that is one reason why so many theologically inclined environmentalists console themselves with process-theology (which allows the progress). Even Chesterton's 'joy without a cause' has been interpreted as the belief that the sky will one day lighten and our trials be past. But Chesterton's point was that only those who do not need to expect a final victory in time will even hold their own. It is not our job to 'save the world', but those who sense God's grandeur and respond to it, may play their part without fear. If we don't, we may instead recall a story of William Faulkner: 'No wonder the ruined woods I used to know don't cry for retribution. The very people who destroyed them will accomplish their revenge.'[27] Nature will provide 'the drunk, or fool or imbecile'. God will repay.

# Notes

1. 'World religions and world orders', *Religious Studies* 26 (1990), pp. 43–57. I am grateful for their comments, and for those of Dundee University Philosophy Society.

2. W. E. Hocking, *Living Religions and a World Faith* (Allen & Unwin: London, 1940), p. 264.

3. I. Kant, 'Perpetual Peace', in H. Reiss (ed.), *Kant's Political Writings* (Cambridge University Press: Cambridge, 1970), p. 114.

4. Daniel 5.4 (JB).

5. H. Belloc, *The Servile State* (Liberty Classics: Indianapolis, 1977; first published 1913), p. 136.

6. R. Kipling, 'The Old Issue' in *Verse 1885–1926* (Hodder & Stoughton: London, 1927), pp. 294f.

7. Kipling, 'A Death-Bed', ibid., p. 283. This is an almost purely malevolent poem, but still has a real moral force.

8. T. Jefferson (1816); cited by A. Koch, *The Philosophy of Thomas Jefferson* (Columbia University Press: New York, 1943), p. 163.

9. E. F. Schumacher, *Small Is Beautiful* (Sphere Books: London, 1974), pp. 44ff.; M. Sahlins, *Stone Age Economics* (Tavistock: London, 1974).

10. W. Blake, 'Marriage of Heaven and Hell' §§5–6 in *Complete Writings*, ed. G. Keynes (Clarendon Press: Oxford, 1966), p. 149.

11. M. Rodinson, *Islam and Capitalism*, tr. B. Pearce (Allen Lane: London, 1974), p. 72; see also B. Nelson, *The Idea of Usury* (University of Chicago Press: Chicago, 1969, 2nd edn).

12. J. N. Findlay, *Language, Mind and Value* (London: Allen & Unwin, 1963), p. 30.

13. The proposal being that any healthy individual might be called, at random, to supply the organs necessary for the survival of the sick. If I must, by law, provide the money (which is my labour) to help needy strangers, and die to defend my country, why is it any odder to demand my body-parts for similarly laudable objectives?

14. See my *From Athens to Jerusalem* (Clarendon Press: Oxford, 1984), p. 85.

15. A. H. Armstrong, 'Some advantages of polytheism', *Dionysius* 5 (1981), pp. 181ff.; p. 184; see *Athens to Jerusalem*, pp. 212ff.

16. C. S. Lewis, *The Abolition of Man* (Bles: London, 1946, 2nd edn), p. 49.

17. A. Toynbee in A. Toynbee and D. Ikeda, *Choose Life* (Oxford University Press: London, 1976), p. 324.

18. H. Richard Niebuhr, *Radical Monotheism and Western Culture* (Harper & Brothers: New York, 1960), p. 126.

19. E. Herbert, *De Veritate*, tr. M. H. Carré (Arrowsmith: Bristol, 1937; first published 1624), p. 76.

20. Herbert, ibid., pp. 83f.

21. See John Baker, *Race* (Clarendon Press: Oxford, 1974): in many ways a deplorable book, but one that accurately represents what many eighteenth- and nineteenth-century scientists thought about the races of humankind, and how 'Christian fundamentalists' opposed them.

22. G. K. Chesterton, *Fancies Versus Fads* (1923), p. 91; cited by M. Canavan, *G. K. Chesterton: Radical Populist* (Harcourt Brace Jovanovich: New York and London, 1977), p. 122.

23. G. K. Chesterton, 'Ballad of the White Horse' in *Collected Poems* (Methuen: London, 1950), p. 233.

24. Chesterton, ibid., p. 257.

25. T. Traherne, *Centuries* 1.31 (Clarendon Press: Oxford, 1960), p. 15.

26. Blake, *Writings*, p. 571. See my 'Where have all the angels gone?', *Religious Studies* 28 (1991), pp. 221–34.

27. W. Faulkner, *Big Woods* (Random House: New York, 1955); cited by M. Sagoff, *The Economy of the Earth* (Cambridge University Press: Cambridge, 1988), p. 145.

# Index